Lively Bible Lessons
for Grades 1-2

Edited by Beth Rowland

Loveland, Colorado

Lively Bible Lessons for Grades 1–2
Copyright © 1992 Group Publishing, Inc.

Credits
Edited by Beth Rowland
Cover designed by Jean Bruns
Interior designed by Dori Walker
Illustrations by Doug Hall

Unless otherwise noted, scriptures are quoted from **The Everyday Bible, New Century Version**, copyright © 1987, 1988 Word Publishing, Dallas, Texas 75039. Used by permission.

Library of Congress Cataloging-in-Publication Data
Lively Bible l;essons for grades 1-2 / edited by Beth Rowland.
     p.   cm.
     ISBN 1-55945-098-3
     1. Christian education of children.   2. Bible crafts.
I. Rowland, Beth. II. Group Books (Firm)
BV1475.2.L58 1992
268'.432--dc20   92-19504
                                             CIP

13 12 11 10 9 8 7 6 5 4   04 03 02 01 00 99 98 97 96 95

Printed in the United States of America.

CONTENTS

Part 3: A Lively Look at Celebrations

INTRODUCTION

Welcome to a resource filled with lively, active Bible lessons for children in first and second grade. Here are fun meetings that'll hold your kids' attention and teach self-esteem-building, friendship-boosting, faith-developing topics.

In *Lively Bible Lessons for Grades 1–2*, Sunday school teachers, vacation Bible school teachers, after-school program directors and any leader of young children will find 20 simple-to-follow lessons that combine lively learning, colorful art projects and scrumptious snacks.

The book is divided into these three parts:

● **Part 1: A Lively Look at My Faith**—Children are interested in God, the church and their developing faith. Faith-building topics include forgiveness, our father God, walking with Jesus, heaven, prayer, the Bible and missionaries.

● **Part 2: A Lively Look at My Relationships**—This section helps children look past themselves to others. Topics include cooperation, compromise, disappointment, kindness, obedience and serving homeless people.

● **Part 3: A Lively Look at Celebrations**—People of all ages love to celebrate special occasions. This section offers Bible lessons and celebrations for New Year's, Valentine's Day, Earth Day, back to school, Halloween, Thanksgiving and Christmas.

THE LIVELY BIBLE LESSONS

The lessons in *Lively Bible Lessons for Grades 1–2* each contain at least six activities. Each activity lasts no longer than 12 minutes. The activities are fast-paced for children with short attention spans. Each lessons is divided into the following elements:

● **Introduction**—One or two paragraphs that give an overview of the lesson's topic.

● **A Powerful Purpose**—A short statement of the lesson's objective, telling you what children will learn.

● **A Look at the Lesson**—An outline including activity titles and estimated completion times. These times may vary depending on your class size.

● **A Sprinkling of Supplies**—A list of all items you'll need for the lesson.

● **The Lively Lesson**—Quick, active, reflective, scripture-based activities. Lessons start with an opening experience to set the mood for the upcoming lesson. Kids experience the topics through active learning using their senses of hearing, seeing, smelling, tasting and feeling.

Lessons include participation Bible stories, games that reinforce biblical truths, action songs to familiar tunes, art projects and snacks.

● **Handouts**—All necessary handouts are included. They're easy to use and you have permission to photocopy them for local church use.

Enjoy *Lively Bible Lessons for Grades 1–2*. Use and adapt the Bible lessons for any gathering of children. Watch kids develop self-esteem, meet new friends and grow in their faith. And have fun teaching topics in an active, lively and meaningful way!

PART 1:
A LIVELY LOOK
AT MY FAITH

GOD IS MY FATHER

Knowing they have a heavenly father can make children feel protected and cared for. Many children have known the loving care of earthly fathers and can easily comprehend God as a caring father.

For other children, "father" isn't a pleasant term. Some children may never see their fathers. Some fathers have mistreated their children.

Use this lesson to introduce children to their loving, caring heavenly father—God. And redefine the term "father" for those children who haven't had a good experience with their earthly fathers.

A POWERFUL PURPOSE

Children will learn to recognize the ways their heavenly father takes care of them.

A LOOK AT THE LESSON

1. Fatherly Qualities (5 to 10 minutes)
2. Fish or Snake? (5 to 10 minutes)
3. It's a Child (5 to 10 minutes)
4. Baby, Baby (10 to 12 minutes)
5. God's Snacks (up to 5 minutes)
6. In Any Other Language (up to 5 minutes)
7. Thanks for Being a Dad (up to 5 minutes)

A SPRINKLING OF SUPPLIES

Gather men's dress-up clothes, small prizes, a Bible, photocopies of the "Heavenly Birth Certificate" handout, crayons, tempera paint, flat pans, wet washcloths, hard-boiled eggs, healthy snacks, fruit juice, paper cups and napkins.

THE LIVELY LESSON

1. Fatherly Qualities

(You'll need men's dress-up clothes such as old shoes, jackets, shirts and ties.)

Throughout this lesson, be sensitive to children who don't have fathers living with them or children whose fathers treat them unkindly. Help these children learn that God is a father who will never leave and who will always treat them with kindness and love.

Invite kids to put on one or two items of the dress-up clothing that fathers wear. Give them several minutes of playtime to act like dads. Encourage responses by asking questions such as "How do fathers talk?" "What do fathers do?" "How do fathers walk?" and "What do fathers like?"

Have children sit in a circle.

Ask:

● **Are dads always perfect?**

Say: **Our fathers are human, and sometimes they make mistakes just like we make mistakes sometimes. Today we're going to talk about a special father who is perfect. We call God our heavenly father because he lives in heaven. God is** perfect—he'll always love us and take care of us.

2. Fish or Snake?

(You'll need small prizes such as stickers or fun-shaped erasers and a Bible. Make sure you have one prize for everyone in the class plus an extra.)

Keep the prizes hidden from the children by keeping them in your pockets or in a small bag. Hold a prize in each hand, and put your hands behind your back.

Say: **I have some prizes to give out, but you have to choose which hand I'm holding the prize in.**

Ask a child to choose which hand the prize is in. When the child chooses, give him or her the prize.

Ask:

● **Was it hard to pick which hand had the prize in it?**

● **Did you think I might have a bad prize in one of my hands?**

● **How would you've felt if I lied to you and told you I had prizes but really didn't?**

Say: **Sometimes when we talk to God, we're afraid that God won't give us what we need. It's hard to trust God sometimes. But the Bible says that if we ask our heavenly father for something good, he won't give us a bad gift. This is what the Bible says.**

Read Matthew 7:9-11 in an easy-to-understand translation, or read this paraphrase: **If your children ask you for bread to eat, would you give them a rock? If your children ask for fish to eat, would you give them a snake? Even though you earthly fathers aren't perfect, you know how to give good things to your children. But God, the heavenly**

father, **is perfect. He will always give good things to those who ask for them.**

Ask:

● **Do your dads always give you what you ask for? Why or why not?**

● **Does God always give us what we ask for? Why or why not?**

Say: **Sometimes we ask for things we don't need. And sometimes we ask for things that aren't good for us, like asking to eat ice cream for supper every night. God is a perfect and loving father. The things God gives us are good for us. God would never do anything to hurt us.**

3. It's a Child

(You'll need photocopies of the "Heavenly Birth Certificate" handout, crayons, tempera paint in flat pans and wet washcloths for cleanup.)

Say: **When babies are born, parents get a special piece of paper that tells about the birth. It's called a birth certificate. Let's make heavenly birth certificates to remind us that God is our heavenly father.**

Distribute the "Heavenly Birth Certificate" handouts and crayons. Have kids fill in their names on the certificates, and help any children who have trouble. Then have the children decorate the certificates. Help children dip their fingertips into tempera paint and roll their fingertips across their certificates to make fingerprints. Set the certificates aside to dry.

Say: **The Bible says everyone who believes in Jesus can be a child of God. It also says God makes us his children because he loves us so much. Let's learn about God's love for us.**

4. Baby, Baby

(You'll need a hard-boiled egg for each child and crayons.)

Say: **Let's play a game to learn how God takes care of his children. Decorate your egg to look like a baby. Then pretend your egg is a real baby and take care of it.**

Give kids each a hard-boiled egg and have them decorate it with crayons. Then give them several minutes to take care of their eggs. Ask questions such as "What will your baby need?" "How will you know if your baby is hungry?" "What will you do if your baby is cold?" and "How will you know if your baby is sick?"

Afterward, ask:

● **How did you feel as you cared for your baby?**

● **How do you think God feels when he cares for you?**

● **Do you think God is as careful with you as you were with your baby?**

Say: **Because God is a perfect father, he knows the best way to take care of us. God takes care of us because he loves us.**

5. God's Snacks

(You'll need healthy, natural snacks such as cut-up vegetables. You'll also need fruit juice, paper cups and napkins.)

Say: **God loves us so much he made us his children and takes care of us. One of the things he does to take care of us is giving us healthy food to eat.**

Serve the healthy snacks. As you eat, have children tell you about how God has taken care of them.

6. In Any Other Language

Have children sit down in an open area of the room.

Ask:

● **What do you call your earthly father?**

Say: **Children in every country have special names for their fathers. You may call your father "Daddy." A Japanese child might call his or her father "Chichi." A German child might say "Papa." In the Bible, Jesus called God "Abba." Let's sing a song to our heavenly father in all these languages.**

Lead children in singing "Father, I Adore You." You can find this song in *The Group Songbook* (Group Books). Each time you sing a new verse, insert the other-language words for "father": daddy, chichi, papa and abba.

7. Thanks for Being a Dad

Close with this prayer: **Father God, thank you for taking care of us. We know you are a perfect father. You love us and you'll always take care of us. Amen.**

by Christine Yount

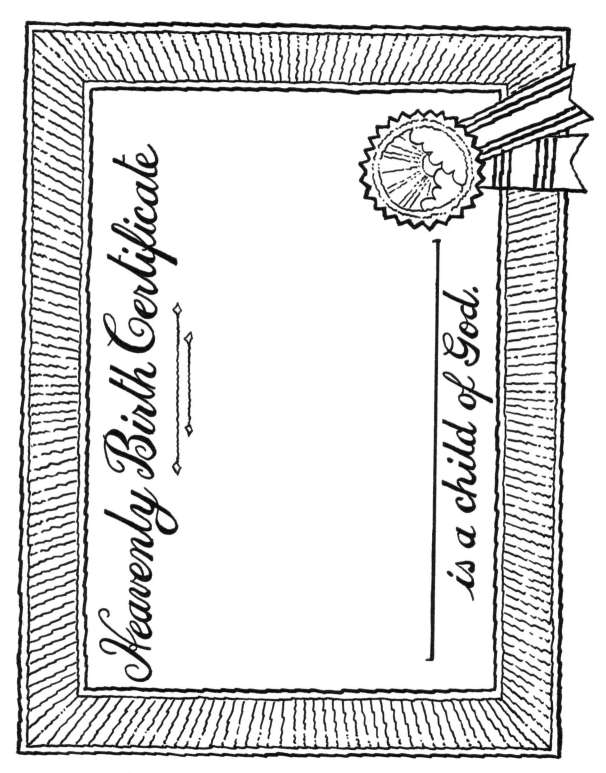

Heavenly Birth Certificate

_____ is a child of God.

GOD'S FORGIVENESS GIFT

orgiveness involves not only our relationships with others but our friendship with God. Jesus teaches us how to forgive others and how to receive forgiveness for our wrongs.

Use this lesson to teach children God forgives and they need to forgive, too.

A POWERFUL PURPOSE

Children will learn to ask forgiveness and to give forgiveness to others.

A LOOK AT THE LESSON

1. Clean Forgiveness (5 to 10 minutes)
2. 70 Times 7 (5 to 10 minutes)
3. Jumpin' for Jesus (up to 5 minutes)
4. As White as Ice Cream (5 to 10 minutes)
5. Forgiveness Song (up to 5 minutes)
6. Hand Hugs (up to 5 minutes)

A SPRINKLING OF SUPPLIES

Gather a handkerchief, disappearing ink, chalk, a chalkboard, jump-ropes, vanilla ice cream, banana slices, marshmallow topping, bowls, spoons and napkins.

THE LIVELY LESSON

1. Clean Forgiveness

(You'll need a handkerchief and a bottle of disappearing ink from a magic store. Before class, test how long you have to wait for the ink to disappear. If you can't find disappearing ink, use a sheet of paper and the Crayola markers that come with the magic "erasing" marker.)

Gather kids in an open area and sit down. Say: **Pretend you're this handkerchief. You're all nice and clean, just like this handkerchief is. But sometimes, we do things that are wrong.**

Ask:

● **What are some of the wrong things we do?**

As a child says a wrong thing we might do, have him or her put a drop of ink on the handkerchief.

Say: **Each time we do something wrong, we make ourselves dirty, just like this ink makes a dirty blotch on the handkerchief.**

Put the handkerchief aside where kids can't see it. Ask questions to keep the discussion going long enough to give the ink time to disappear.

Ask:

● **How does it make you feel**

when you do wrong things?

● **What happens when you do wrong things?**

Say: **When we do wrong things, it makes God sad because we can't go to live with God if we've done bad things.**

But God did a wonderful thing for everyone in the world when he sent his son! Jesus came to earth so that we can be forgiven for all the wrong things we do. Being forgiven means he washes all the dirt away so we look brand new again.

Bring out the handkerchief. The ink should have disappeared.

Say: **Because God loves us, we can be cleaned of all the wrong we do. When we do something wrong, and we're sorry we did it, all we have to do is ask God to forgive us. He promises that he will.**

2. 70 Times 7

(You'll need chalk and a chalkboard.)

Say: **Sometimes, we're not the ones who do wrong. Sometimes people hurt us. They might hurt our feelings or they might do something mean like cutting in front of you in line.**

Ask:

● **When has someone hurt you?** Encourage children to share their experiences.

● **How did you feel when that person hurt you?**

● **What did you do?**

Say: **We can forgive others when they hurt us. Peter asked Jesus how many times should we forgive others when they do wrong things to us. Peter asked, "Should I forgive someone seven times?"**

Choose a volunteer from the class and have him or her make seven chalk marks on the chalkboard.

Say: **Jesus said, "You should forgive someone 70 times seven." Let's put marks on the chalkboard to show how many times we should forgive people. Seventy times seven means we'll need seventy rows of seven chalk marks.**

Have children take turns putting rows of seven chalk marks on the chalkboard. Continue making marks until you have 70 rows of seven or until your chalkboard is full.

Say: **This is a giant number!**

Ask:

● **How can we keep track of how many times we forgive someone?**

Say: **Keeping track of forgiving people would take a lot of time. When Jesus said we should forgive people 70 times seven, he meant we should always forgive people, no matter how many times they hurt us.**

3. Jumpin' for Jesus

(You'll need a jump-rope for every three to four children and lots of space. Do this outside if you can.)

Have the children break up into groups of three or four and give each group a jump-rope. Have kids take turns turning the jump-rope. Teach the following jumping rhyme and see how many times kids can "forgive":

Jumpin' for Jesus, that's what I want to do.
Forgiving others, that's what we should do.
How many times can I forgive?
1-2-3-4-5-6-7-8-9-10 . . .

4. As White as Ice Cream

(You'll need vanilla ice cream, banana slices, marshmallow topping, bowls, spoons and napkins.)

Say: **The Bible says that when God forgives us, he makes us clean. God says when we're forgiven, we're so clean that we're as white as snow. Let's eat a snack that'll remind us how clean we are when God forgives us.**

Serve ice cream sundaes made with vanilla ice cream, banana slices and marshmallow topping.

As you eat, ask children to tell you about a time when they were forgiven or when they forgave someone.

5. Forgiveness Song

Sing this song to the tune of "Three Blind Mice." As children sing, have them pretend to dust themselves off.

Forgiveness.
Forgiveness.
God makes me clean.
God makes me clean.
When I do something bad God
 still cares for me,
He wants me to say that
 I'm sorry,
And try not to do the same
 bad thing,
He'll forgive me.
He'll forgive me.

I'll forgive.
I'll forgive.
God wants me to.
God wants me to.
When someone hurts me I'll
 say "That's okay,
God forgave me; I'll forgive
 you, too,"
The Bible tells us to forgive
 our friends,
So I'll forgive.
So I'll forgive.

6. Hand Hugs

Have kids stand in a circle and hold hands. Say: **God forgives us because he loves us. When we forgive others, we show we love them.**

Ask:

● **How do you feel when you forgive someone?**

● **How do you feel when someone says to you, "It's okay. I still want to be friends with you"?**

Say: **Being forgiven and forgiving others makes us feel good. Forgiving spreads God's love to everyone. Let's spread some "hand hugs" around our circle to show how much we love each other. See if you can watch the love go around the circle.**

Squeeze the hand of the child to your right. That child should squeeze the hand of the next person, and so on around the circle.

Remind kids to squeeze gently. They're passing love, so they don't want to hurt each other. If someone squeezes too hard, use the teachable moment to practice forgiveness. Ask the child whose hand was hurt, "How did you feel when (Child's name) squeezed too hard?" Ask the squeezer, "How did you feel when you squeezed (Child's name) hand so hard?" Ask the child to apologize. Ask the other child to forgive. Have them exchange a hand hug that shows love.

When the hand hug comes back to you, pray: **God, you love us so much you forgive us when we do wrong. Help us to remember to say we're sorry. And help us to remember to forgive others when they hurt us. Amen.**

by Elaine Friedrich

WALKING WITH JESUS

F ollowing Jesus every day is as challenging for children as it is for adults. It's a lot easier to take control of our own lives than it is to follow and obey someone we can't see. Children need to learn that walking with Jesus brings joy and peace.

Use this lesson to teach kids to trust that Jesus is faithful to guide them safely through life.

THE POWERFUL PURPOSE

Children will learn how to follow Jesus.

A LOOK AT THE LESSON

1. Barefoot Maze (5 to 10 minutes)
2. Immediate Following (5 to 10 minutes)
3. Quickly Follow (5 to 10 minutes)
4. Follow Your Partner (10 to 12 minutes)
5. Sticking With Jesus (up to 5 minutes)
6. Follow Pictures (up to 5 minutes)
7. Help Us to Follow (up to 5 minutes)

A SPRINKLING OF SUPPLIES

Gather a rope, blindfolds, magazine pictures of things that might be hard to give up, a Bible, a small object, various classroom items to build an obstacle course with, sandwich cookies, milk, paper cups, napkins, paper and crayons or different-color markers.

THE LIVELY LESSON

1. Barefoot Maze

(You'll need a rope and a blindfold.)

Lay out a long rope around the room in a winding pattern. As children arrive, have them to take off their shoes. Have children take turns wearing the blindfold and walking on the rope as though it were a tightrope.

After each child has had a turn, ask:

● **Was it easy or hard to walk on the rope? Explain.**

● **What would have made it easier to walk on the rope?**

Say: **Sometimes it's hard to know what to do. Just like it was hard to follow the rope when you couldn't see, sometimes it's hard to know the difference between right and wrong.**

Ask:

● **Have you ever had trouble deciding what the right thing to do is?**

Encourage children's responses. A child might say he went to the kitchen where his mom had just baked cookies. She wasn't there and he had to decide if he should eat one without permission. Or a child might say she had to decide whether to tell a lie or to tell the truth and hurt a friend's feelings. If kids are stumped by this question, mention these examples or mention something from your own experience.

Then say: **Following Jesus helps us know what to do and what not to do. Today we're going to learn how to follow Jesus.**

2. Immediate Following

(You'll need magazine pictures of things that might be hard to give up, such as a pet, a house, toys, a television, parents and friends. You'll also need a Bible.)

Spread out the pictures on the floor in front of the children.

Ask:

● **Suppose you were told you had to give up these things—which would be the hardest to give up?**

● **Would it be easy to give up any of these things?**

Open the Bible to Matthew 4:17-22. Say: **There were some men in the Bible who were asked to give up everything to follow Jesus. Listen to this story about them.**

Tell kids that every time they hear the words "fish," "fishing" or "fishermen," they should act like they're reeling in a fish. Demonstrate this action for kids who might not know what the word "reel" means.

Say: **One day, Jesus started to preach. He told the people, "Change the way you think and the way you live because the kingdom of heaven is near."**

Jesus walked by the Sea of Galilee and saw two brothers named Simon and Andrew. The brothers were fishermen. They threw a big net into the water. When they pulled the net back in, it was full of fish.

Jesus said to Simon and Andrew, "Come and follow me. I'll make you fish for people."

Simon and Andrew put down

their nets and immediately followed Jesus.

Jesus kept on walking by the Sea of Galilee. He saw two more brothers named James and John. They were sitting in a boat with their father, repairing their fishing nets.

Jesus said, "Come, follow me."

And James and John immediately put down the nets and left their boat and their father to follow Jesus.

After the story, ask:

● **How do you think Simon, Andrew, James and John felt about giving up everything to follow Jesus?**

● **Why do you think they followed Jesus instead of staying where they were?**

● **Have you ever felt like you had to give something up to do what makes Jesus happy?**

Say: **It was probably hard for these men to leave everything behind, but they were quick to obey Jesus when he asked them to follow. Let's play a game about being quick to follow.**

3. Quickly Follow

(You'll need a small object such as a rock or a small toy.)

Have kids stand in a circle. Teach children this song to the tune of "Ring Around the Rosie."

**When we walk with Jesus,
We do what makes him happy.
Jesus, Jesus,
We'll follow him.**

Tell kids that as they sing the song, they'll pass the small object around the circle as fast as they can. When the song is over, everyone must watch the person who's holding the object and be quick to follow his or her motions. The child with the object may do actions such as making a funny face, twirling around several times or doing a few jumping jacks. Play until all the children have had a chance to choose an action for the class to follow. Then have kids sit down.

Ask:

● **What did you have to do in order to follow the actions quickly?**

● **How is that like being quick to follow Jesus?**

● **What kinds of things make Jesus happy?**

Say: **To follow Jesus, we need to pay attention to what he wants us to do. We can do that by spending time with Jesus when we pray and study the Bible. And we can learn in church what things make Jesus happy.**

4. Follow Your Partner

(You'll need enough blindfolds for half the class to have one and classroom items such as chairs, tables and building blocks.)

Have the kids design and construct an obstacle course in your room. The course can be built with anything you have in your classroom. Use chairs, tables and building blocks to create the course. Help kids decide how each obstacle is to be dealt with. For example, kids may have to get through the "boulder field" of building blocks without stepping on any. They may have to crawl through an "underground cave" by crawling under a table. Encourage kids to use their imaginations.

When the course is complete, have kids form pairs and decide which partner will be the leader and which partner will be the follower. Blindfold the followers. Pair by pair, have the leaders guide the followers through the obstacle course. Don't give them any

directions on how to do it; let them figure out the easiest way to guide their partners.

After each pair has gone through the course, have the followers take off their blindfolds. Gather the class in an open area and sit down.

Ask the leaders:

● **Was it easy or hard to guide your partner through the obstacle course? Explain.**

Ask the followers:

● **Was it easy or hard to follow your partner's directions? Explain.**

Say: **Following your partner through the obstacle course is like following Jesus. We have to trust that Jesus will guide us, even though we don't know everything that's going to happen. Jesus knows what's going to happen, just like the leaders could see what the obstacle course was like. We can trust that Jesus will guide us safely.**

If any of the leaders in your class purposely led their partners astray on the obstacle course, use the opportunity to talk about how Jesus is trustworthy even though people sometimes aren't.

5. Sticking With Jesus

(You'll need sandwich cookies, milk, paper cups and napkins.)

Pass out the cookies and cups of milk. While kids are eating, twist apart a cookie and show kids how the cream sticks to the cookie. Say: **The cream part of this cookie is like Jesus. He'll stick by us no matter what happens. We're like the cookie part. Sometimes we stick with Jesus. But sometimes we don't want to stick with him.** Show kids the cookie without the cream.

Ask:

● **When is it hard to stick with**

Jesus?

● **How do you think Jesus feels when we say we don't want to do what makes him happy?**

● **What happens when we do things that make Jesus unhappy?**

Say: **It's hard to always follow Jesus. But we know that when we follow Jesus, he protects us and takes care of us.**

6. Follow Pictures

(You'll need paper and crayons or different-color markers.)

Distribute paper. Have kids each choose one color crayon or marker and draw a winding path on their paper. Then have them choose another color and follow as closely as possible the original winding path. Have them continue adding colors until they have a winding rainbow.

As the kids are drawing, ask:

● **What can you do this week to**

WINDING RAINBOW

follow Jesus?

7. Help Us to Follow

Close in prayer, thanking Jesus for sticking to us and asking him for help in following him every day.

by Janel Kauffman

HEAVEN: GOD'S SPECIAL PLACE

Heaven's an abstract concept that's not easy for concrete-thinking first- and second-graders to understand. Some think heaven's up in the clouds. Others wonder where heaven is on a cloudless day. Still others aren't quite sure what heaven is.

But, heaven's important to the Christian faith. Use this lesson to help your first- and second-graders learn about heaven and see that it's God's special place.

A POWERFUL PURPOSE

Children will learn that God loves them so much he has a special place—called heaven—where they'll be with him forever.

A LOOK AT THE LESSON

1. Building a Special Place (5 to 10 minutes)
2. All Cozy Together (up to 5 minutes)
3. What'll We Do in Heaven? (5 to 10 minutes)
4. A Special Drawing (5 to 10 minutes)
5. John's Picture of Heaven (5 to 10 minutes)
6. A Heavenly Snack (up to 5 minutes)

7. Thanks for Heaven (up to 5 minutes)

A SPRINKLING OF SUPPLIES

Gather chairs, sheets, blankets, a flashlight, a Bible, art supplies, a bag of marbles or glass beads, pearl buttons or an inexpensive strand of faux pearls, gold foil or wrapping paper, angel food cake or heavenly hash ice cream, plates or bowls, and forks or spoons.

THE LIVELY LESSON

1. Building a Special Place

(You'll need chairs, sheets and blankets.)

Welcome children as they arrive. Ask them to start building a tent large enough for the entire class using chairs, sheets and blankets. Encourage children to use chairs to prop up the sides of the tent and also the middle portion of the tent. Let the children decide how to construct the tent. Give guidance if conflicts arise or if children have trouble making the tent stand.

2. All Cozy Together

(You'll need a flashlight.)

Once children have finished the tent, have them gather under the tent together. Use the flashlight to provide light if the tent is dark. Encourage children to sit close together.

Ask:

● **How does it feel to sit so close together in this tent?**

● **How do you feel when you sit close to the people you love most?**

Say: **We know God loves us. Because he loves us, God made a special place for us called heaven. And just like we're all together in this special place, we can be together with God in God's special place called heaven. Christians go to live with God in heaven after they die. They'll live with God forever.**

3. What'll We Do in Heaven?

(You'll need a Bible.)

Open the Bible to Matthew 5:12.

Say: **The Bible has something good to say about God's special place called heaven. In Matthew 5:12, it says, "Rejoice and be glad. You have a great reward waiting for you in heaven."**

Ask:

● **What do you think the reward will be?**

● **What do you think we'll do in heaven?**

Say: **The Bible says that in heaven there won't be any sadness or crying or pain. Everything will be brand new. In heaven, we'll sing songs to God. Now let's all crawl out of this special place and sing songs to practice for when we go to heaven.**

Sing your class's favorite songs about God. Some possibilities are "Alleluia," "Rejoice in the Lord" and "I Will Call Upon the Lord." They're all in

The Group Songbook (Group Books).

4. A Special Drawing

(You'll need an assortment of art supplies such as construction paper, tissue paper, crayons, chalk, markers, glitter, yarn, ribbon, fabric scraps, glue, scissors, watercolors and paintbrushes.)

Have children create pictures of what they think their special place called heaven looks like. If children are stumped, encourage them to incorporate some of the parts of their special rooms or treehouses into their pictures.

When kids are finished with their pictures, have them find a partner and tell each other about their pictures of heaven.

Say: **The Bible tells us a little bit about what heaven will be like but not enough so we know exactly what it looks like. It'll be fun when we get there to see if any of you made a picture that looks just like heaven.**

5. John's Picture of Heaven

(You'll need a Bible, a bag of marbles or glass beads, pearl buttons or an inexpensive strand of faux pearls, and gold foil or wrapping paper. You'll also need a flashlight.)

Open the Bible to Revelation 21. Say: **God showed Jesus' friend John what heaven looks like. He wrote about it in a book called Revelation that's in the Bible. John says heaven is like a city made with precious jewels, pearls and gold.**

Show kids the supplies and say: **Let's build heaven with these things.**

Help kids build a flat, two-dimensional heaven. Let kids decide how it should be designed. You may want to use modeling clay to hold the building materials in place.

When "heaven" is built, shine the flashlight on heaven and say: **Look how all the jewels shine. The Bible says that in heaven there won't be a sun because God is so bright he lights up all of heaven.**

6. A Heavenly Snack

(You'll need a "heavenly" snack such as angel food cake or heavenly hash ice cream, plates or bowls, and forks or spoons.)

Say: **Let's eat this heavenly snack to remind us of how special heaven will be.**

While you eat, have kids tell you what they want to do when they get to heaven or what they want to ask God when they get to heaven.

7. Thanks for Heaven

Gather children in an open area and pray: **God, thank you for making a beautiful home for us called heaven. Amen.**

by Jolene Roehlkepartain

TALKING TO GOD

A dults often choose carefully what to say in prayers, but prayer does not follow a magical formula and there aren't restrictions on when and where we can pray. Children may not understand how easy prayer really is.

Use this lesson to teach first- and second-graders that prayer is simply talking to God. Teach them that God wants to talk with them about everything, no matter how big or small the issue. In this lesson, children will learn how to pray, and they'll learn that God answers prayer.

A POWERFUL PURPOSE

Children will learn they can pray any time to a God who answers their prayers and takes care of them.

A LOOK AT THE LESSON

1. Prayer Categories (5 to 10 minutes)
2. Prayer Puzzles (5 to 10 minutes)
3. Daniel Prayed (5 to 10 minutes)
4. Song Praises (5 to 10 minutes)
5. Daily Bread (up to 5 minutes)
6. Prayer Pictures (5 to 10 minutes)
7. Prayer Tree (up to 5 minutes)

A SPRINKLING OF SUPPLIES

Gather a playground ball, scissors, photocopies of the "Prayer Puzzle" handout, an envelope, a Bible, classroom supplies, bread, butter, a knife, paper, crayons or markers, pipe cleaners and a small, artificial Christmas tree or a tree limb.

THE LIVELY LESSON

1. Prayer Categories

(You'll need a playground ball.)

Have kids stand in a circle in an open area of the room. If your room is carpeted, you may want to play this game outside on a hard surface.

Say: **Today we're going to talk about prayer. One way to pray is to say thank you to God. Let's thank God for all the things he's made. When I mention a category, I'll bounce the ball to someone in the circle. That person has to think of something God has made that fits in that category and yell it out. Then that person bounces the ball to someone else.**

As you play each category, continue until the ball is bounced to everyone in the circle. It's okay if a child can't think of an answer or wants to repeat an answer. But if there are too many repeats, whisper a new idea in children's ears.

● Thank you, God, for food...
● Thank you, God, for nature...
● Thank you, God, for colors...
● Thank you, God, for animals...
● Thank you, God, for toys...

Say: **There are lots of things to thank God for. Let's find out some more about prayer.**

2. Prayer Puzzles

(You'll need photocopies of the "Prayer Puzzle" handout and an envelope.)

Make photocopies of the "Prayer Puzzle" handout and cut out the pieces. You should make one photocopy for every three children. Put the "missing" pieces in an envelope.

Form groups of three. Give each group a photocopy of the puzzle and have the group put it together. When they find there's a puzzle piece missing some groups may come to you and ask about it. Give these groups one of the missing pieces you've put in the envelope. Other groups may not mention the missing piece to you. Don't give these groups the missing piece.

Have the children sit on the floor in an open area of the classroom.

Ask:

● **What happened when you tried to put your puzzle together?**

● **What did you think when you found a puzzle piece was missing?**

● **What did you do when you found a puzzle piece was missing?**

● **What happened when you asked (didn't ask) for the missing puzzle piece?**

Say: **There are times when we don't know what to do, or we need something we don't have. We can ask God to give us the answers we need or to give us the things we need. Since God always does what's best for us, we know he'll answer our prayers. Sometimes he doesn't give us what we ask for, but he always gives us what we need.**

3. Daniel Prayed

(You'll need a Bible.)

Gather children in an open area of the room and sit down. Tell them that every time they hear the word "Daniel" they should kneel and fold

their hands as though they were praying, then sit down again.

Open your Bible to Daniel 6. Say: **A long time ago, the people who lived in Israel were captured and had to live in a country called Babylon. They had to live there for many years.**

The Babylonians didn't believe in the same God the Israelites believed in. Many Israelites still worshiped God even though they lived in a country where the people didn't pray or worship the same God.

Daniel was one of the Israelites who still worshiped God. He was a smart man and the king gave him an important job. This made some Babylonians angry. They thought the best jobs should go to Babylonians not Israelites.

They wanted the king to give Daniel's job to someone else, but the king wouldn't do it because Daniel did his job well.

The men convinced the king to make a law that said everyone who lived in Babylon had to pray to the king. They couldn't pray to anyone else.

Even though Daniel knew about this new law, he still prayed to God three times every day.

The king found out and had to punish Daniel. He had Daniel thrown into a cave with lots of lions. Then he had a stone put over the opening of the cave so Daniel couldn't get out.

The king left Daniel there overnight, but he couldn't eat or sleep because he was so worried about Daniel.

The next morning, the king hurried to the lions' cave. He called

out, "Daniel, has your God saved you from the lions?"

Daniel answered, "Yes, I'm still alive. My God has taken care of me."

The king threw the evil men who had accused Daniel into the lions' home and the lions gobbled them up.

Then the king wrote a letter to the world that said, "Daniel's God lives forever. He has rescued Daniel from the lions."

From that day on, Daniel could pray whenever he wanted to.

4. Song Praises

(You'll need classroom items such as blocks, pencils and boxes of crayons.)

Send kids around the room to find noisemakers. Anything they can find in the classroom that will make noise is okay. Be sure to mention if there are any items that can't be used. For example, anything that might break or anything that belongs to a different group that uses your room should be off limits.

When everyone has found a noisemaker, say: **The Bible says one way to pray is to make a joyful noise to God. Let's sing a song and make noise for God.**

Have children make noise while they sing a lively praise song such as "This Is the Day," "Great Is the Lord" or "I'm Gonna Sing, Sing, Sing." These can all be found in *The Group Songbook* (Group Books).

5. Daily Bread

(You'll need bread and butter.)

Say: **When Jesus prayed, he thanked God for giving him daily bread. When Jesus said that to God, he was saying thank you to God for giving him all the things he needed. Let's eat some bread and butter now as a reminder that God gives us what we need.**

As children eat have them tell each other about prayers God has answered for them and about the needs they have that God has met. Children may say God has given them food, parents and friends.

6. Prayer Pictures

(You'll need paper and crayons or markers.)

Say: **God wants to know what we need. Telling him what we need is one way to pray to God. God also wants to know what's happening in our lives and how we feel. Even though he knows everything, he likes to talk with us.**

Distribute paper and crayons or markers. Have children draw pictures of the things they want to tell God or of things they need from God.

Have children tell two other children in the class about the picture they've drawn.

7. Prayer Tree

(You'll need the prayer pictures, pipe cleaners and a small, artificial Christmas tree or a small tree limb that's been "planted" in a pot of dirt.)

Have children fold their prayer pictures accordion-style. Then give them each a pipe cleaner, and have them lay it in one of the middle "valleys" of the folded paper.

Put the tree in the middle of the room and have the children bring their prayer pictures and stand in a circle around the tree.

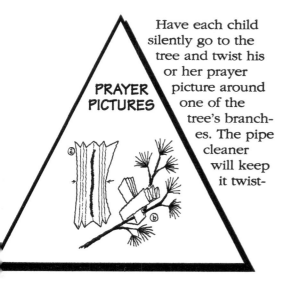

PRAYER
PICTURES

Have each child silently go to the tree and twist his or her prayer picture around one of the tree's branches. The pipe cleaner will keep it twist-ed around the branch.

After each child has put his or her prayer on the tree, pray: **God, thank you for being someone we can talk to. You know what makes us happy and what makes us sad. You know what each person in this class has put on our prayer tree. Please answer these prayers in a way that will help us. Amen.**

PRAYER PUZZLE

This is
the
"missing"
piece.

GOD'S WORD TO ME

The things children learn now become the foundation that everything in their lives will be built on. That's why it's important to teach children about the Bible now instead of waiting until they're old enough to understand it all.

Use this lesson to teach first- and second-graders that the Bible is God's special gift to us that teaches us how to live.

A POWERFUL PURPOSE

Children will learn that God's special gift to them, the Bible, teaches them how to live.

A LOOK AT THE LESSON

1. A Dark Path (5 to 10 minutes)
2. What's in the Bible (up to 5 minutes)
3. A Man Named Paul (up to 5 minutes)
4. B-I-B-L-E (up to 5 minutes)
5. Bible Pictures (5 to 10 minutes)
6. Food for Thought (up to 5 minutes)
7. Thank You for the Book (up to 5 minutes)

A SPRINKLING OF SUPPLIES

Gather a flashlight, small candies, a Bible, photocopies of the "What's in the Bible" handout, crayons or markers, raisins, dates, nuts, whole wheat bread or matzo bread, honey, napkins, paper cups and milk. You'll also need access to a room that can be made completely dark.

THE LIVELY LESSON

1. A Dark Path

(You'll need access to a room that can be made completely dark, a flashlight and a bag of small candies.)

Have kids line up in a straight line. Stand at the front of the line and lead kids in a game of Follow the Leader. Tell them there's a prize for those who can follow you through the entire game. Wind your path through the room and vary your steps so that kids will need to pay close attention to follow you. But don't make it too hard. Everyone should be able to keep up.

Then lead kids into the darkened room. Continue the game in the darkened room long enough for kids to get frustrated. They'll probably complain that they can't see you well enough to follow your actions. In the dark room, choose movements such as tiptoeing so that kids don't get hurt in the dark. Also, make sure there's nothing in the room that will trip or injure a child.

Then turn on the flashlight and continue the game. Lead children back into the classroom. Declare all the children winners and give each one a small piece of candy.

Gather the children in an open area of the room and sit down.

Say: **It's hard to find our way**

when it's dark. You had trouble following me when we went into the
dark room. But as soon as I turned
on the flashlight, you could all see
what to do.

Ask:

● **Have you ever been someplace
where it's so dark you couldn't see
where you were going?**

Encourage children's responses.
They may mention spending the night
in a strange house, going into the
basement at home or being outside on
a cloudy night. Ask:

● **How do you feel when you
can't see which way to go?**

Say: **Not knowing where to go is
scary. Sometimes it's hard to tell
the difference between right and
wrong. It can be as scary as being
in a dark room and not knowing
which way to go. But the Bible is
like a light that helps us know what
to do, just like the flashlight helped
all of you to know how to follow
the leader.**

2. What's in the Bible

(You'll need a Bible.)

Put the Bible on a chair on one side
of the room. Put the empty chair on
the other side of the room.

Say: **The Bible tells us many things
that help us know what to do. I'm
going to read a list of things that
might be in the Bible. If you think
I've read something that's in the
Bible, clap your hands twice, then
point to the chair with the Bible. If
you think I've read something that's
not in the Bible, clap your hands
twice and point to the other chair.
Here's the list:**

**Love the Lord your God with all
your heart.**

The story of David and Goliath.

Teenage Mutant Ninja Turtles.

**Put on your coat before going
outside.**

The story of Moses.

**Treat others the way you want to
be treated.**

Eat all your broccoli.

Be kind to each other.

Don't lose your mittens.

Obey your mom and dad.

Gather kids in an open area and sit
down. Tell kids which things from the
list are from the Bible. Watch for children who feel bad if they didn't know
the right answers. Assure them the
activity wasn't a test and you didn't
keep score.

Ask:

● **How did you decide what
things from the list are in the Bible?**

Say: **When we come to church,
we learn what's in the Bible. The
things we learn about in church
help us know how to follow God.**

**Many years ago, God told people
to write messages to all the people
in the world. God wanted people to
know he loves them. These messages were collected, and that's what
makes up the Bible. Listen to this
story about one of the men who
wrote part of the Bible.**

3. A Man Named Paul

(You'll need a Bible.)

Tell children to pretend they're
writing every time they hear the word
"Saul" or the word "Paul." Say: **God
trusted many people to write down
what he wanted to tell people. One
of those people was Saul. But at
first, he didn't even believe that
Jesus was God's son.**

**Saul was a leader in the syna-
gogue. When he was alive, they
didn't have the New Testament yet.**

He studied hard in school and knew more about the Old Testament than anyone. But Saul didn't believe that Jesus was God's son. In fact, he was mean to people who believed in Jesus.

One day, Saul was traveling to the city of Damascus to arrest the Christians there. He thought they were going against God. While he was traveling, a bright light flashed. He was so scared that he fell to the ground. He heard a voice say, "Saul, Saul. Why are you hurting me?"

Saul asked, "Who are you?"

The voice said, "I am Jesus, the one you are hurting. Get up and go into the city. Someone there will tell you what to do."

Saul got up from the ground and opened his eyes. But he couldn't see. The people Saul was traveling with led him into the city. For three days, he couldn't see.

Then, Jesus told Ananias to go see Saul. Ananias was scared because he knew that Saul wanted to kill the Christians. But he went anyway.

Ananias put his hand on Saul and said, "Jesus sent me so that you may see again and be filled with the Holy Spirit."

Immediately, Saul could see again. He was baptized, and he started telling people about Jesus. He believed that Jesus is God's son, and he was sorry for the mean things he did to the Christians.

Saul and his friend Barnabas went on long missionary trips to tell people about Jesus. When Saul started to go on these trips, he changed his name to Paul. Paul and Barnabas went all over the world telling everyone about Jesus. **Paul wrote letters to the people he visited so they would know that God loves them and so they would know how to follow God. Many of these letters are in the Bible.** Show the children some of Paul's books in the Bible.

4. B-I-B-L-E

Lead kids in singing this song to the tune of "Bingo":

There is a book to show me how
To live right every day.
B-I-B-L-E,
B-I-B-L-E,
B-I-B-L-E,
The Bible is its name, oh.

Filled with stories, songs and
**   prayers**
That help me make good
**   choices.**
B-I-B-L-E,
B-I-B-L-E,
B-I-B-L-E,
The Bible is its name, oh.

God gave the book to light
**   my way**
And tell me that he loves me.
B-I-B-L-E,
B-I-B-L-E,
B-I-B-L-E,
The Bible is its name, oh.

5. Bible Pictures

(You'll need photocopies of the "What's in the Bible" handout and crayons or markers.)

Distribute the handouts and crayons or markers. Have children decorate their Bible covers so that people will know what's inside the Bible. Children might draw a scene from a specific

Bible story or they might illustrate a biblical principle such as kindness. Encourage their creativity by having them tell partners about their pictures.

6. Food for Thought

(You'll need biblical foods such as raisins, dates, nuts, whole wheat bread or matzo bread, and honey. You'll also need napkins, paper cups and milk. Make a trail mix of the raisins, dates and nuts. Cube whole wheat bread or buy a box of matzo bread and serve with honey.)

Serve the snack of different foods from the Bible and milk.

Say: **The Bible tells us that people ate these foods in Bible times.**

As children eat, have them tell you about their favorite Bible story.

7. Thank You for the Book

(You'll need the Bible covers children made in the Bible Pictures activity.)

Gather kids in a circle and have them hold their Bible covers so the rest of the class can see what they've drawn. Begin the prayer. Then go around the circle and have each child finish the sentence by saying what he or she has drawn.

Pray: **God, thank you for giving us the Bible as a special gift. It helps us figure out what we should do. Thank you for . . .** (*Have children each finish the sentence*) **Amen.**

by Elaine Friedrich

WHAT'S IN THE BIBLE

FARAWAY FRIENDS

People all over the world need to learn about Jesus. Children in church may not know that some people have never heard of Jesus.

Use this lesson to teach first- and second-graders that missionaries travel all over the world to tell others God loves them.

A POWERFUL PURPOSE

Children will learn how missionaries spread the good news about Jesus.

A LOOK AT THE LESSON

1. What Do Missionaries Do? (up to 5 minutes)
2. Jesus' Command (up to 5 minutes)
3. Missionary Tag (10 to 12 minutes)
4. A Missionary Song (up to 5 minutes)
5. Missionary Food (up to 5 minutes)
6. Care Packages (10 to 12 minutes)
7. Pray for Our Friends (5 to 10 minutes)

A SPRINKLING OF SUPPLIES

Gather a toy doctors kit, a Bible, a chalkboard, gardening tools, a cassette player, a cassette of Christian music, sliced fruit, a box, care package items, paper, crayons or markers, red construction paper, scissors, masking tape, a map of the world or a globe, and a blindfold.

You'll also need information on a missionary your church or denomination supports and information about the country the missionary serves in.

THE LIVELY LESSON

1. What Do Missionaries Do?

(You'll need a toy doctors kit, a Bible, a chalkboard, gardening tools, a cassette player and a cassette of Christian music.)

Set out the doctors kit, the Bible, the chalkboard and the gardening tools. Play the Christian music.

Give kids a few moments to look at all the items.

Ask:
● **Who uses these items?**
● **What are these items used for?**
● **What do these items have in common?**

Say: **Lots of people use these items every day. Missionaries use all of these items to tell people about God.**

Ask:
● **What do you think these items could tell people about God?**

Say: **Some of these things help people. The doctors kit helps sick people get better, and the gardening tools can help grow food for people. The chalkboard, the music and the Bible can be used to teach people about God. All of these things help missionaries tell people that God cares about them.**

2. Jesus' Command

(You'll need a Bible.)

Open the Bible to Matthew 28. The following story is based on this chapter and Acts 1. Have children sit in a circle as close together as possible.

Say: **After Jesus rose from the dead, he spent several days in Jerusalem with his followers. Then it was time for him to go to heaven to live.**

Jesus and his followers went to a mountain and the followers worshiped Jesus. Jesus said to them, "I have an important job for you. I want you to travel all over the world and tell other people about me. Teach them how to follow me and obey me. Baptize them. And be sure to remember I'll always be with you."

Jesus also told them he would send the Holy Spirit to help them. Jesus said, "Go tell others about me. Tell the people in your town, Jerusalem. Then go to the people in the district of Judea. (Have children scoot back a couple of feet) **Then go farther away to the district of Samaria.** (Have children scoot back a few more feet) **Then go even farther away and tell everyone in the world about me."** (Have kids move back against the walls, standing as far apart as possible)

After Jesus said this, he was lifted up into the air and went to heaven.

Jesus' followers did exactly what Jesus told them to do. They sent missionaries to tell people about Jesus. And today, there are Christians all over the world because of missionaries. But even though missionaries have told people all over the world about Jesus, there are lots of people who've never even heard of Jesus. That's why we still send missionaries today.

3. Missionary Tag

Say: **Let's play a game to see what it's like to be a missionary.**

Choose one child to be the missionary. The missionary must tag each child in the room and say, "God loves you." As each child is tagged, he or she sits down. Tell the children to pretend they don't know that it's a good thing to be loved by God, so they should do everything they can to keep from being tagged.

After everyone has been tagged, ask the missionary:

● **How did it make you feel when nobody wanted to know God loves them?**

Say: **Being a missionary is hard work. And there are many more people in the world than we have in our classroom. It took a long time for** (child's name) **to tag everybody. If** (child's name) **had to tell everyone in the world about Jesus it would take forever. Missionaries do things differently. Let's play the game again to see how missionaries really work.**

Play the game again. Choose another child to be the missionary. Say: **This time when you're tagged you become a missionary, too. After you're tagged, you can tag others and say, "God loves you."**

After the game, ask:

● **What was different about this game?**

● **How did you feel knowing that each time you tagged someone, they'd start helping you tag others?**

Say: **Missionaries know that the best way to get the news to everybody is to teach people how to tell** others about Jesus. It makes the job a lot easier and this way lots of people get to help spread the news about Jesus.

4. A Missionary Song

Lead children in singing this song about missionaries. Sing it to the tune of "My Bonnie Lies Over the Ocean."

**To those who live over
    the ocean,
To people in lands near and far,
To all who will listen and learn,
We send missionaries to say,
"God loves you, God loves you.
He loves you so much that he
    sent his son.
God loves you, God loves you.
And wants to know you love
    him, too."**

5. Missionary Food

(You'll need sliced fruit that children in other countries eat every day such as papayas, mangoes and red bananas and sliced fruit that children in your class eat every day such as apples and pears.)

Say: **Some missionaries go to other countries to tell people about Jesus. Sometimes they have to learn a new language and learn to eat food they're not used to.**

Have kids eat some of the fruit served in other countries.

Ask:

● **What would it be like to go live in another country?**

Say: **Some missionaries stay in their own countries. They may not have to learn new languages or eat different food, but they still tell people about Jesus.**

Have kids eat some of the fruit they're used to.

Ask:

● **What would it be like to be a missionary in your own country?**

6. Care Packages

(You'll need information on a missionary your church or your denomination supports and information about the country the missionary serves in. You'll also need a box and care package items to send to the missionary, such as current magazines, snackfood that isn't available in that country, letters of encouragement written by your class, pictures drawn by your class and a photograph of your Sunday school class.)

Tell children about a missionary your church or denomination supports. Children will be interested in the country the missionary is living in and what the missionary does every day. If you can get a photograph of the missionary, children will have a stronger connection to the missionary.

Say: **When missionaries go to other countries, they miss all the friends and family members they leave behind. Let's send a package to this missionary to show we care about him (or her).**

Help children write letters and draw pictures to send to the missionary. Pack the box with all the items you've collected. If possible, give children an opportunity to bring things from home for the missionary. Collect their items the next time your class meets. Finish packing the box and send it to the missionary.

7. Pray for Our Friends

(You'll need red construction paper, scissors, masking tape, a map of the world or a globe, a blindfold and a marker. Cut a heart from construction paper for each child.)

Hang the map on a wall. Make masking tape loops on the backs of the hearts and give one heart to each child. Have children take turns wearing the blindfold and taping their hearts to countries all over the world. Write the name of the country each child picks on the heart. If they land in the ocean, let them have another chance.

After each heart is placed on the map, pray for the missionaries that go to that country and for the people who live in that country. For example, pray: "Lord, thank you for the missionaries in Panama and thank you for our friends in Panama. Help the missionaries tell everyone there that you love them. Amen."

by Elaine Friedrich

Part 2: A Lively Look at My Relationships

LET'S TEAM UP

Working together is a difficult skill to learn. Even with constant practice, cooperation skills that take a lifetime to refine. First- and second-graders need to know God planned for us to work together.

Use this lesson to teach children how to work together. They'll learn that even though cooperation takes work, it's rewards are worth the effort.

THE POWERFUL PURPOSE

Children will learn that we were created to cooperate.

A LOOK AT THE LESSON

1. Team Balloon (8 to12 minutes)
2. Scavenger Hunt (5 to 10 minutes)
3. Team Art (5 to 10 minutes)
4. The Israelites and the Wall (5 to 10 minutes)
5. Watermelon Puzzles (5 to 10 minutes)
6. Cooperative Prayer (up to 5 minutes)

A SPRINKLING OF SUPPLIES

Gather a marker, a sheet, a balloon, classroom items or nature items, lunch bags, cloth strips, modeling clay, paper grocery bags, two watermelons and a knife.

THE LIVELY LESSON

1. Team Balloon

(You will need a marker, a sheet and a balloon.)

With a marker, draw a line down the center of a sheet widthwise to separate it into two sections. Blow up the balloon and tie it off. Form two teams and have each team line up around one of the sheet sections. It's important to have kids at the ends of the sheet and also around the sides of the sheet.

Have the children hold the sheet waist high and bounce the balloon up and down by moving the sheet. Each team must try to get the balloon to go off the sheet on the opposite side. The children must hold the sheet at all times and can't touch the balloon with any part of their bodies. When the balloon goes off the sheet on one team's side, the other team gets a point.

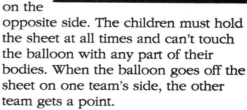

TEAM BALLOON

Play for a couple of minutes or until 5 points are scored.

Then reorganize the teams for round 2. On one team every team member plays. On the other team only the kids along the end of the sheet play. The kids who were stationed on the sides have to stand away from the sheet and can cheer their team on, but they can't play the game.

Play for a couple of minutes or until 5 points are scored.

Have the kids put the sheet down and sit on top of it.

Ask:

● **What made the second game different from the first game?**

● **Was the second game fair?**

Ask the cheerers:

● **How did you feel knowing that you couldn't help your teammates but could only cheer from the side?**

Ask the players of the small team:

● **How did you feel when you had to play against a team with more players?**

Say: **It was important to work together to win this game. When some team members couldn't play, this game was much harder for the rest of the team. It was also hard for those who couldn't play. They wanted to work together to win the game. God wants us to work together, too. Today we'll talk about how we can cooperate.**

2. Scavenger Hunt

(You'll need small items that can be found in your classroom or outside, lunch bags and cloth strips.)

Before class, put 5 to 10 small items in each lunch bag. You'll need one lunch bag for every two children. Choose items that are easy to find such as a crayon, a glue bottle and a wooden block or a dandelion, a pebble and a leaf.

Have children find partners. Tie each pair's inside legs together with one or two cloth strips as you would for a three-legged race. Give each pair a lunch bag.

Send them on a scavenger hunt. Tell them they must find the items in their bag and add another one of each item to their bag. For example, if they have a pebble in their bag, they must find another pebble to put in their bag. When they finish, they should have two of each item.

Give them three to five minutes to find everything in their bags, then call them back and have them sit in an open area of the classroom.

Ask:

● **Was it easy or hard to work together? Explain.**

● **What did you have to do to find all your items?**

● **What would've made this game easier?**

Say: **Sometimes figuring out how to work together can be hard. It can feel funny to work together and sometimes we think it'd be easier to do things by ourselves. But God has created us to cooperate. When we learn how to work together it can be fun and we can get more done.**

3. Team Art

(You'll need modeling clay.)

Give each child a hunk of modeling clay. Assign each child a body part to make such as bodies, legs, arms, heads, ears and faces. If you have more than six children, form groups of no more than six. Give the children a few minutes to turn their hunk of clay into body parts.

Ask:

● **What could you do if you only had legs? arms? a face? ears? a body?**

Say: **The Bible tells us that even our bodies cooperate. We need to** have all of our body parts to do all the fun things we want to do. We can cooperate with each other just like our body parts cooperate.

Ask:

● **What things can we do when we cooperate that we can't do by ourselves?**

Say: **Let's put our body parts together to show that we want to cooperate.**

Form an assembly line and have each child add his or her body parts to the body to form a clay person.

4. The Israelites and the Wall

(You'll need large paper grocery bags.)

Say: **Our story takes place at a city named Jericho. The people of Jericho built a huge wall to protect their city. Let's use these grocery bags and work together to build a city wall.** Have children help you open the bags and stand them on their open ends. Space the bags about six inches apart. Put five bags on the bottom row, four in the second row, and so on, centering each bag over a gap in the previous row.

Then say: **The people of Israel had a job to to. Their job was to conquer the land of Palestine so God's people could settle there. To do that, they had to conquer the city of Jericho. When the people of Jericho saw the army coming, they locked all the doors in the city wall—nobody went in or out.**

The people of Israel wondered how they could get by this great walled city. Then God gave them some unusual instructions.

Instead of telling them to attack, God told them to march around the city one time every day for six

days. Seven priests carried trumpets. Some priests carried the ark of the covenant, which was a big box with the Ten Commandments in it. The soldiers marched, too, and carried their weapons.

Lead the children in a march around the wall. As you're marching, say: **The people worked together to follow God's instructions. Once a day for six days, the priests and the soldiers marched around the wall. Then they went back to their camp. On the seventh day, they marched around the city seven times.** (Have the children march around the wall seven times) **Then the priests blew their horns, and Joshua commanded everyone to shout.** Have the children make trumpeting sounds, and then have them shout, "For the Lord and for Joshua!"

As the children shout, kick one of the bottom bags so the wall tumbles down.

Say: **And just like that, the walls of Jericho fell down and the army of Israel won a great victory!**

Ask:

● **How do you think the Israelites felt when the city walls fell down?**

Say: **The Israelites were willing to work together to follow God's directions even when the directions were unusual. Because they worked together and obeyed God, they won the battle. When we cooperate with each other, God can help us, too. Cooperating can make everything a lot easier.**

5. Watermelon Puzzles

(You will need two watermelons and a knife.)

If possible, do this activity outside. If you do it inside, put plastic tablecloths on the tables. Cut the watermelons in unusual shapes so it will be challenging to put them back together. Cut each one in about 10 pieces.

Form two groups. Have kids wash their hands. If any of the children have colds or unprotected scrapes, give them supervisory jobs within their group instead of watermelon-handling jobs. Give each group one of the watermelons and tell them to work together to put it back together.

After the watermelons have been put together, let each child choose a piece of watermelon to eat. Enjoy the snack.

6. Cooperative Prayer

Have kids stand in a circle. Have them all turn to their right and scratch the back of the person in front of them. After a minute or two, have them turn around and scratch the back of the person in front of them. Then have them face the center and hold hands.

Pray: **Thank you, God, for giving us each other. It's good to have friends to cooperate with. Teach us to help each other and cooperate with each other even when it's hard. We know that you've created us to work together. Amen.**

by Janel Kauffman

LET'S COMPROMISE

Children face conflict all the time. Rubbing shoulders with brothers, sisters, parents, teachers and friends every day creates endless possibilities for bickering and fighting.

God knows we'll disagree with each other. How we handle conflict is what's important. Use this lesson to help children learn how to cope with conflict in a way that pleases God.

A POWERFUL PURPOSE

Children will learn how to work out conflict with each other.

A LOOK AT THE LESSON

1. Climate for Conflict (10 to 12 minutes)
2. Tug of War (5 to 10 minutes)
3. A Christian Fight (5 to 10 minutes)
4. All Stirred Up (5 to 10 minutes)
5. What If? (5 to 10 minutes)
6. Tug-of-War Snacks (5 minutes)
7. Tug a Prayer (up to 5 minutes)

A SPRINKLING OF SUPPLIES

Gather toys or a home center, masking tape, a rope, a Bible, construction paper, scissors, baby food jars, markers, glitter, sequins, water and a pull-apart snack such as licorice or fruit leather.

THE LIVELY LESSON

1. Climate for Conflict

(You'll need toys, such as blocks, or a home center. If your classroom does not have a home center, bring in plastic dishes and old pots and pans. Paint four circles on a piece of plywood to make a stove. Use a plastic tub for a sink. Cover a classroom table with a tablecloth to make a dining room table.)

As children arrive, lead them to areas with toys such as blocks. Or lead them to a home center. Allow children to play for five to 10 minutes. Watch for conflicts. As children play, don't scold them when they disagree. Conflict itself isn't bad.

Instead, use the conflicts to teach children how to communicate honestly and arrive at a mutually acceptable compromise. For example, if Jim won't let Rebecca play with the blocks, don't insist they play side by side. Ask them how it feels to disagree. Ask them for ideas on how to solve the problem. Explore each idea to see if it's workable and to see what the result would be. Let the children decide what the best solution is. Affirm the children for their ideas and their willingness to find solutions. Also affirm children who deal with conflict positively.

If no conflicts occur, have the children sit in an open area and ask questions such as "What would've happened if Jim wouldn't let Rebecca play with the blocks?" "How would Rebecca feel?" and "What could they do to solve their problem?"

2. Tug of War

(You'll need masking tape and a rope.)

Form two teams and have each team stand on one side of a masking tape line in the middle of the room. Clear chairs and tables from this area. On "go," have team members tug on their end of the rope to pull the other team across the center line.

Don't let children tug so hard they hurt each other. Tell them not to jerk the rope so that no one gets hurt.

Afterward, gather children in an open area and have them sit down.

Ask:

● **Who won this game?**

● **How did you feel when your friends lost this game?**

● **When you're angry with a friend, is it ever like having a Tug of War? Why or why not?**

● **Think about the last fight you had with a friend, a brother or a sister—who won the fight?** Allow time for children to tell about their fights.

Say: **Today we're going to talk about "compromise." Compromise means to meet in the middle. In our Tug of War, it would've been a compromise if both teams had chosen to cross the line at the same time. Then both teams would've won the game. In a fight, compromise means both people have to give up something in order for both sides to win. Let's look at two people in the Bible who disagreed and see how they compromised.**

3. A Christian Fight

(You'll need a Bible.)

Open the Bible to Acts 15:36-41. Say: **Paul and Barnabas traveled all over the Roman Empire telling people how much God loved them. When they went to a town, they went first to the synagogue where the Jewish people worshiped God. They told the people about how Jesus came to the earth and died for them. Then they went to the marketplace where people bought their food, and they told the people there about God's love.**

Paul and Barnabas stayed with the people for a while, teaching them about God and how to be Christians. They traveled from town to town, telling people about Jesus and starting new churches. Sometimes, they went back to visit the churches they started.

One day, Paul said, "We should go back to visit all the towns where we preached God's message. Let's visit all the Christians to see how they're doing. When we see how they're doing, we can encourage them and know how to pray for them."

Barnabas wanted to take John Mark with them to help. But Paul disagreed. John Mark had been their helper earlier but left them when they came to a town called Pamphylia. Paul didn't think that John Mark was a good helper. He didn't think he could trust John Mark to stay and help.

Paul and Barnabas argued about what to do. Finally, they compromised. They decided that Barnabas would travel with John Mark and Paul would travel with a man named Silas. So they split up. Both Paul and Barnabas visited the churches to encourage the people even though they didn't travel together anymore. Because they compromised and split up, they visited more churches than they would have if they'd stayed together.

Ask:

● **Does it surprise you that people in the Bible disagreed? Why or why not?**

● **Is it bad to disagree? Why or why not?**

● **How did Paul and Barnabas compromise?**

Say: **Let's see what the Bible says about disagreeing.**

Read aloud Ephesians 4:26.

Say: **The Bible doesn't say it's a sin to be angry and disagree. It just says to work out your problems before the day is over. Paul and Barnabas worked out their problem. And God wants us to work out any problems we have with each other.**

4. All Stirred Up

(You'll need construction paper, scissors, baby food jars with lids, markers, tape, glitter, sequins and water. Before class, cut out construction paper circles the size of a baby food jar lid.)

Say: **Let's make a craft that'll remind us to work out our problems in a way that makes God happy.**

Give kids each a clean baby food jar and lid. Have children each write on a circle of construction paper the words, "When you are angry, do not sin." Have them tape the paper to the jar lid. Then have children put glitter and sequins inside the jars. Help kids fill their jars with water and tightly shut the lids.

Ask:

● **How do you feel when you're angry?**

Have the children shake their jars. Ask:

● **Do you ever feel like your insides are shaken up when you're mad at someone?**

Have kids let their jars settle down. Then say: **God wants us to settle down and work out our problems with others when we're angry. Then our insides will calm down. Let's practice working out our problems with each other.**

5. What If?

Form pairs by having children grab the hand of someone close to them.

Read aloud the situations below, and have the pairs come up with as many solutions as they can think of. Then have each pair act out one of their solutions for the class. After each solution is presented, ask about the result. For example, ask, "How was the conflict solved when Sarah and Jan decided to make more dessert?" or "How does that make Sarah and Jan feel?"

Here are the situations:

You're eating lunch at your partner's house, and there's only one dessert left. Both of you want it.

Your families go to a park for a picnic. You brought some bikes along, but there aren't enough for you and your partner to ride at the same time.

You just found out your partner told your parents a lie about you.

6. Tug-of-War Snacks

(You'll need thin licorice ropes or Fruit by the Foot fruit leather cut in 1-foot pieces.)

Pass out one piece of licorice or fruit leather to each child, but have them wait to eat it.

Have children tell about conflicts they've had and how they felt. Then have them pull apart the snack.

Say: **Disagreeing can make us feel torn apart, just like when we tear**

this snack or when we played Tug of War. But when we compromise and solve our conflicts, everyone feels better.

Have the children eat their snack and talk about how they solved their conflicts or how they can solve the next conflict they have.

7. Tug a Prayer

(You'll need a rope.)

Form two teams and have each team hold on to opposite ends of the Tug-of-War rope on either side of the masking tape line.

Close with this prayer: **God, sometimes we disagree and we fight.** *(Have teams pull on the rope)* **But you've asked us to solve our problems before the day ends.** *(Have both teams put the rope down, line up facing each other along the masking tape line and shake hands)* **Help us remember to love each other and solve our problems quickly.** *(Have kids each hug the person they're standing across from)* **Amen.**

by Christine Yount

WHEN I'M DISAPPOINTED

Nobody's perfect. Kids know that all too well. Sometimes their parents disappoint them. Or their grandparents. Or their friends. Or you.

Often, kids' expectations for people are too high. But children can learn to have realistic expectations and to forgive people who don't meet their expectations.

Use this lesson to help children learn how to cope with a world filled with imperfect humans—including themselves.

A POWERFUL PURPOSE

Children will learn to forgive when people disappoint them.

A LOOK AT THE LESSON

1. Can We Build It? (5 to 10 minutes)
2. So High (5 to 10 minutes)
3. Disappointment (up to 5 minutes)
4. Chicken Out (up to 5 minutes)
5. Rooster Pocket (up to 5 minutes)
6. Forgiveness Tastes Good (up to 5 minutes)
7. Wipe It Out (up to 5 minutes)

A SPRINKLING OF SUPPLIES

Gather building blocks, small candies, chalk, a chalkboard, a heavy object, a Bible, photocopies of the "Rooster" handout, crayons, blunt-tip scissors, a stapler, a chalkboard eraser, small pencil erasers, banana slices, grapes and napkins.

THE LIVELY LESSON

1. Can We Build It?

(You'll need building blocks.)

Guide children to an area with building blocks. Form two teams, and have each team race to build the highest tower. Say: **We're going to race to see which team can build the tallest tower. But be careful. If your tower falls, your team is out of the race.**

Encourage children to build their towers higher and higher. It's important that their towers fall. They need to experience disappointment to learn about it.

If children want to play it safe and don't build their towers tall enough for them to fall, talk about being afraid of being disappointed. Ask questions such as "Why did you decide not to build your tower any higher?" "How would you have felt if your tower had fallen?" Then say, "If your tower had fallen, you would've been disappointed. When you stopped building, you tried to make sure your tower wouldn't fall so you wouldn't be disappointed. But sometimes we're disappointed by things other people do and by things we can't stop from happening."

After at least one of the towers falls, ask:

● **How did you feel when the tower fell?**

● **Do you know what "disappointment" means?**

Say: **Disappointment is being**

unhappy because things didn't happen the way you wanted them to happen.

Ask:

● **Did you feel disappointed when the tower fell?**

● **Have you ever wanted something for your birthday and you didn't get it?**

● **How did you feel?**

● **Have you ever planned to go somewhere special and at the last minute something happened so you didn't get to go?**

● **How did you feel?**

If children can't relate to these examples, ask them to tell you about a time they were disappointed.

Say: **You felt disappointed. Sometimes other people mess up and disappoint us. Sometimes we mess up and disappoint others. And sometimes things just don't turn out the way we want them to. Today we're going to talk about a time Jesus was disappointed and what he did about it. We'll learn what we can do when we're disappointed.**

2. So High

(You'll need a bag of small candies, chalk, a chalkboard and a heavy object.)

Tell children you're going to have a contest. If anyone can pass any of the three tests, they'll get a piece of candy as a prize.

Draw a mark on the chalkboard or use tape to mark the wall—so high that children cannot reach it even if they jump. Have children take turns trying to touch the mark without climbing on a chair or table.

Then have children take turns trying to lift the heavy object—one that is impossible for them to lift.

Then ask children to spell "supercalifragilisticexpialidocious."

Afterward, have children sit in a circle on the floor. Sit with them and say: **I'm disappointed because I wanted to share this candy with you.**

Ask:

● **How did you feel when you didn't pass any of the tests?**

Say: **You couldn't do these things because they are impossible for most of you. I expected too much from you. If I expected you to be able to drive a car, I'd be disappointed because you don't know how to drive. Or if I expected you to run 10 miles, I might be disappointed because that's too far. Sometimes we're disappointed in people we love because we expect too much. We want them to do more than they can do.**

Tell a story from your own life of a time you were disappointed. For example, you might tell about an expensive gift you wanted for Christmas and didn't get because your family couldn't afford it.

Say: **Since everyone tried so hard, let's share the candy anyway.**

Give each child a piece of candy.

3. Disappointment

(You'll need chalk and a chalkboard that children can reach. If you don't have a chalkboard that children can easily reach, paint a smooth piece of plywood with chalkboard paint. You can find chalkboard paint in most hardware or craft stores. Put the painted plywood on the floor or on a table, and let children gather around it.)

Have children draw pictures or write words on the chalkboard that tell about a time when they felt disappointed.

After children are finished with their drawings, ask:

● **How does disappointment make you feel?**

● **What do you do when you're disappointed?**

Say: **Let's find out about a time when Jesus was disappointed.**

Save the chalkboard drawings for the Wipe It Out activity.

4. Chicken Out

(You'll need a Bible.)

Open the Bible to Mark 14–15. Tell kids to listen for the word "rooster." Every time they hear the word "rooster," they can stand up and say "cock-a-doodle-do" and then sit down.

Say: **Jesus and his disciples were gathered on the Mount of Olives one night. Jesus said, "Tonight each of you will wonder if you should believe in me. The Bible says it'll happen."**

But Peter said, "Everyone else may wonder, but not me. I will always have faith in you."

Jesus answered, "Peter, I'm telling the truth when I say this. Tonight, you will say three times that you don't even know me. Then the rooster will crow."

Peter said, "I'll never say that. I'll always believe in you, even if I have to die with you."

Later that night, soldiers came and arrested Jesus. They took him to the house of the high priest. Peter stood in the garden outside the priest's house. It was very cold so some people made a fire to keep warm. Peter came close to the fire and one of the priest's servants said, "You were with that man Jesus."

Peter said, "I don't know what

you're talking about. I was never with Jesus."

Peter left the garden and stood by the gate. The servant said to the people standing with Peter, "This man was with Jesus."

But Peter said again, "I promise that I don't even know the man."

A little while later some other people said to Peter, "We know you are one of the men who followed Jesus."

Peter said a third time, "I don't even know Jesus."

Immediately a rooster crowed. Then Peter remembered what Jesus had said to him. He knew he disappointed Jesus. Peter left the high priest's house and started to cry.

Ask:

● **How did Jesus know Peter would disappoint him?**

● **Why did Peter disappoint Jesus?**

● **Have you ever disappointed someone you love? Explain.**

● **How did you feel when you disappointed that person?**

Say: **Jesus knew everything about Peter, and he knew that Peter was human. That's why Jesus didn't expect Peter to be perfect. Jesus understood that Peter wanted to please Jesus but that Peter would fail.**

5. Rooster Pocket

(You'll need photocopies of the "Rooster" handout, crayons, blunt-tip scissors, a stapler, chalk, a chalkboard, a chalkboard eraser and small pencil erasers.)

Give each child a "Rooster" handout. Have children color and cut out their roosters and pockets. Help children staple the pockets to the roosters.

Say: **When Peter heard the rooster crow for the third time, he** knew he had disappointed Jesus. But that's not the end of the story. Jesus forgave Peter and still loved him.

Draw a face with a big frown on the chalkboard or with a pencil on paper. Erase the frown and draw a smile as you say: **When Jesus forgave Peter, Jesus erased Peter's sadness and made Peter happy again. Sometimes people disappoint us—they don't do what we want them to do. We need to forgive them just as Jesus did. We need to stop being mad at them. When we forgive people, we erase the disappointment— we forget it ever happened.**

Give each child an eraser to place in their rooster pocket to remind them to forgive others when others disappoint them.

6. Forgiveness Tastes Good

(You'll need banana slices, grapes and napkins.)

Have children arrange fruit on their napkins to look like sad, disappointed faces. Have them tell about a time when they were disappointed. Then tell them to say silently, "I forgive you" to the person who disappointed them.

Say: **When you forgive someone, it means you'll act as though they never did the thing that disappointed you. Forgiving people makes us happy and it makes them happy.**

Have kids change their sad, disappointed faces to happy, forgiving faces. Then enjoy the snack.

7. Wipe It Out

(You'll need the chalkboard with the disappointment drawings from the Disappointment activity and a chalkboard eraser.)

Gather children around the chalkboard. Pray: **Thank you, God, for forgiving Peter when he disappointed you. Thank you for forgiving us when we disappoint you. Help us forgive people who disappoint us. Help us to erase the hurt we feel.** Give each child the opportunity to use the eraser to erase his or her disappointment drawing from the chalkboard and to silently say, "I forgive you." Then say: **Amen.**

by Christine Yount

ROOSTER

Photocopy this handout for children to color and cut out.

KEYS TO KINDNESS

First- and second-graders know the world isn't fair. They also have a keen sense of justice. Yet, children are likely to respond to injustice in kind rather than in kindness.

God commands us to actively love those who don't love us. Children need effective skills to help them show kindness to the people they encounter daily. Use this lesson to help children learn how to respond with love.

A POWERFUL PURPOSE

First- and second-graders will learn how to be kind to people who aren't kind to them.

A LOOK AT THE LESSON

1. Make a Face (up to 5 minutes)
2. Hurting to Healing (up to 5 minutes)
3. Feelings, Feelings (10 to 12 minutes)
4. Kind Words for Tough Times (up to 5 minutes)
5. A Kind Song (up to 5 minutes)
6. Showers of Kindness (5 to 10 minutes)
7. A Warm, Kind, Fuzzy Snack (up to 5 minutes)
8. A Fuzzy Challenge (up to 5 minutes)

A SPRINKLING OF SUPPLIES

Gather paper, crayons, a marker, adhesive bandages, a Bible, cotton balls, cotton candy and wet washcloths.

THE LIVELY LESSON

1. Make a Face

Have children find partners. Tell children to make these faces at their partners as you call them out: **growl, smile, stick out your tongue, laugh.**

Children will probably giggle during this activity. After the game, say: **This was fun because we were just playing a game. But sometimes people make mean faces at us. Sometimes people hurt us.**

Throughout this lesson, be sensitive to children who may suffer from abuse. In those situations, it's not wise for a child to be kind back. Encourage the option of telling a teacher or another adult when someone hurts them so bad that they need help.

Ask:
● **When has someone been mean or unkind to you?**
● **How does it feel when someone is really angry with you and yells at you?**
● **How does it feel when someone is angry with you even when you haven't done anything wrong?**
● **How does it feel when a friend smiles and laughs with you?**

Say: **Today we're going to talk about what God wants us to do when others treat us unkindly.**

2. Hurting to Healing

(You'll need paper, crayons, a

marker and adhesive bandages. Use a marker to write "kindness" on a bandage for each child.)

Give each child a sheet of paper and some crayons. Have children draw pictures of how they feel when someone is mean to them. Encourage children to choose colors they think are "mean."

When children finish, say: **When people are mean to us, it hurts. But when we are kind to the people who are mean to us, it can make us feel better, and sometimes it even helps the mean person to be kind to us.**

Give children each an adhesive bandage, and have them put the bandage over their "mean" picture.

Say: **Let's find out how kindness works.**

3. Feelings, Feelings

Have children find partners. Say: **A verse in the Bible says, "Make sure that nobody pays back wrong for wrong, but always try to be kind to each other and to everyone else"** (1 Thessalonians 5:15, NIV). **Let's think of some ways to be kind, even when others are mean to us.**

Have partners take turns acting out the mean role in each of the following situations. Have the other partner act out a kind response. Give kids a few minutes to role play after you read each situation.

● **Pretend you're on the playground during recess. A mean classmate says, "Those clothes are ugly. I'd never wear anything that funny looking."**

● **Pretend you're walking to school. A mean bully comes up to you and says, "Give me your lunch money. If you don't, I'll pound**

your head in."

● **Pretend you're in the library. Someone else makes a really loud noise, but the cranky librarian thinks it's you and says, "If I hear one more sound out of you, you'll have to leave the library and never come back."**

● **Pretend you're playing with your friend in the living room at your house. Your friend accidentally knocks your mom's favorite vase off a shelf and breaks it. When your mom asks what happened, your friend blames it on you. You get punished.**

Some kids may have difficulty thinking of kind responses. That's okay. Kindness isn't easy. Don't make those who have trouble with this activity feel bad. Let them learn from others' ideas. If all the pairs are stumped by any of these situations, offer suggestions of kind responses and let the kids act those out.

After each situation, ask the "kind" partner:

● **How did you feel when your partner was mean to you?**

● **What did you do after your partner was mean to you?**

● **How did it feel to be kind instead of mean?**

Ask the "mean" partner:

● **How did you feel when your partner did something kind for you instead of something mean?**

Say: **It's easier to be mean when others are mean to us. But it makes everybody feel better when we do kind things. And, it makes God happy, too.**

4. Kind Words for Tough Times

(You'll need a Bible.)
Have kids sit on the floor. Say:

Doing kind and loving things is important to God. Listen to what Jesus says.

Read Luke 6:27, 31-36 in an easy-to-understand version of the Bible, or read this paraphrase: **Listen to what I say. Love your enemies. Do good things for the people who don't like you. Treat other people the way you want to be treated. If you do loving things only for the people who love you, you're just like everyone else. Even bad people do that. But I say do good things for people who do bad things to you. Then you will have a big reward. You will be acting like children of God because God is kind to people who are bad. Be kind just like God is kind.**

Ask:

● **Why is it hard to be kind when others are mean to us?**

● **What happens when we're mean to mean people?**

● **What happens when we're kind to mean people?**

Say: **It's a lot harder to be kind to people who hurt us. But it helps us to be friends instead of enemies.**

5. A Kind Song

Lead the class in singing this song to the tune of "I've Been Working on the Railroad."

God says to always treat with kindness,
Those who are mean to me.
God says to always treat with kindness,
Though it's very hard to do.
I'll do my best to act in loving,
Kind and thoughtful ways.
God says to always treat with kindness,
I will not let him down.

I'll be so kind, I'll be so kind,
I'll be so kind to all I know.
I'll be so kind, I'll be so kind,
God will show me how.

6. Showers of Kindness

(You'll need cotton balls.)

Have kids stand in a circle. Choose a volunteer to stand in the middle. Give handfuls of cotton balls to each child in the circle. Have them think of kind things they can say to the child in the middle. Then on "go," have the children yell out kind things. For each kind thing they yell, they can gently toss a cotton ball at the child in the middle. After the child in the middle has been "showered with kindness," let another child stand in the middle. Continue until everyone has had a turn.

Have children help pick up the cotton balls.

7. A Warm, Kind, Fuzzy Snack

(You'll need cotton candy and wet washcloths for cleanup.)

Say: **Sometimes we call kind words warm fuzzies because they make us feel good inside. Let's enjoy a warm-fuzzy snack.**

Tear off a piece of cotton candy for each child. As you hand a piece to each child, say a kind thing to each one. For example, say, "Katie, thank you for your bright smile."

Cotton candy can be found in many discount stores. If it's not available in your area, have the children decorate iced cookies with colored coconut. As the children eat their cookies, have them say something kind about the children on both sides of them.

8. A Fuzzy Challenge

(You'll need cotton balls.)

Have kids stand in a circle. Give each one a cotton ball. Tell them to think of one kind thing they each can do or say for a member of their family. When they do the kind things for their family members, have them give those people the cotton balls as warm fuzzies. Be sure to ask about their kind deeds the next time you meet.

Close with this prayer: **God, we learn so much from you. Because you are kind, we want to be kind, too. Remind us to do kind things for people, even the people who are mean to us. Amen.**

by Jolene Roehlkepartain

CHOOSE TO OBEY

From the first "No!" kids heard their parents say, they've understood the concept of obedience—if you don't obey, you'll have to pay the consequences. And for first- and second-graders, paying the consequences isn't usually much fun.

Children can learn, however, that they can choose whether or not they obey.

Use this lesson to help children understand the importance of obedience and teach them to make good choices.

A POWERFUL PURPOSE

Children will learn why they should obey and understand that they can choose to obey.

A LOOK AT THE LESSON

1. I Can Choose (5 to 10 minutes)
2. School Rules (8 to 10 minutes)
3. Simon Says (5 to 10 minutes)
4. Here I Am (5 to 10 minutes)
5. Choosy People (up to 5 minutes)
6. Pray to Obey (up to 5 minutes)

A SPRINKLING OF SUPPLIES

Gather various craft supplies, a Bible and several different snacks.

THE LIVELY LESSON

1. I Can Choose

(You'll need various craft supplies, such as paints and paintbrushes, crayons, markers, paper, Popsicle sticks, ribbon, blunt-tip scissors, tissue paper, glue, tape and glitter.)

Show children the craft supplies and tell them to make a craft. Don't give the children any other instructions. As they work on their crafts, watch children closely to discover any children who are frustrated with this activity. Encourage them, but don't give them any direction.

Have kids display their crafts. Compliment each one.

Then ask:

● **How did you feel when I didn't tell you how to make your craft?**

● **Would this craft have been more fun to make if I had explained how to do it?**

Say: **Sometimes it's fun to choose for ourselves what we want to do. And sometimes, it's better to follow instructions. Today we're going to talk about how to decide when it's important to do what we want and when it's important to follow instructions.**

2. School Rules

Have kids help you set up the chairs and tables to resemble a schoolroom. Have them sit in the chairs.

Ask:

● **What does obedience mean?**

Say: **Obedience is doing what the person in charge tells you to do.**

Ask:

● **What would it be like if we decided not to obey?**

● **What happens when you don't follow the rules?**

Say: **Let's play school and see what it'd be like if people decided not to follow rules.**

Choose a volunteer to play the teacher. Tell the students they get to choose whether or not they follow the rules. Give the children several minutes to play school. To get things started, you may need to whisper rules in the teacher's ear such as "Sit and read to yourselves," "Get in line to go to an assembly" or "Don't talk."

If the students seem reluctant to disobey, encourage them by whispering disobedient actions in their ears such as "Read out loud," "Run around the room instead of getting in line" or "Talk loudly." But let them decide what they want to do.

After several minutes of playtime, ask:

● **How did you feel when you decided to break the rules?**

● **What is school like when people don't follow the rules?**

● **What is school like when people do follow the rules?**

Say: **No matter where we are, we can choose whether we want to obey the rules or not. It's best to obey God, teachers and parents because they make rules to help us and protect us.**

3. Simon Says

Have children help you put the chairs against the wall to form an open space in the middle of the room.

Say: **We're going to play a game where you have to decide which rules you should obey.**

Play this variation of Simon Says.

You play Simon. Before each command you give, say "Simon says." Let kids decide, though, which rules they'll obey. If they choose to obey, have them do the command. If they decide not to obey, they must sit down until they hear a command they want to obey.

Use these commands:

Run around the room two times.

Hop up and down eight times.

Eat three crayons.

Give two people a big hug.

Climb to the top of the church building and jump off.

Do six jumping jacks.

Do 250 sit-ups.

Draw happy faces in the air.

Take my car keys and drive my car around the parking lot.

Kids will probably choose not to eat the crayons, jump off the church building, do 250 sit-ups or try to drive your car. If some children want to try, instead of letting them, ask questions such as "What would eating crayons taste like?" "What would happen if you did jump off the top of the church building?" or "What would happen if you drove my car around the parking lot?" It won't hurt them to attempt 250 sit-ups, but they'll tire long before they're finished. If they choose to obey the sit-up command, don't force them to finish.

Have kids sit down in the open area.

Ask:

● **Why did you decide not to obey sometimes?**

● **Is there ever a time in real life when you shouldn't obey?**

If children can't think of a time when they should disobey, ask what they would do if a stranger offered them a ride home.

Say: **Most of the time, rules are made to help us. But if someone tells you to do something that will hurt you, it's okay not to obey.**

4. Here I Am

(You'll need a Bible.)

Have children lie on the floor. Explain to them that they're going to listen to a story about a boy who listened to and obeyed God. Every time they hear the word "Samuel," they are to jump up and say, "Here I am." Then they should lie down again.

Open the Bible to 1 Samuel 3. Tell this story, pausing after you say "Samuel" to give children time to jump up and say, "Here I am."

Say: **Samuel** (*pause*) **was a boy who lived in the temple with a priest named Eli. He helped Eli, and Eli taught him all the important things he needed to know. Samuel** (*pause*) **knew it was important for him to obey Eli so he'd learn.**

One night they were in bed sleeping. Samuel (*pause*) **heard a voice say "Samuel"** (*pause*)**. He thought Eli was calling him, so he got up and quickly ran to Eli and said, "Here I am. You called me."**

But Eli said, "I didn't call you. Go back to bed."

So he went back to bed.

A little later he heard the voice again. It called "Samuel" (*pause*)**.**

He got up and ran to Eli's bed again and said, "Here I am. You called me."

But Eli said, "No, I didn't call you this time, either. Go back to bed."

So he went back to bed again. He was puzzled because he didn't know who was calling him. Then, it happened again. The voice said

"Samuel" (*pause*).

He got up a third time and ran to Eli's bed. This time Eli realized God was calling Samuel (*pause*)**. So Eli said, "Go back to bed. The next time God calls, say, 'Speak, Lord. I'm your servant and I'm listening.' "**

Samuel (*pause*) **went back to bed. God spoke again and said, "Samuel, Samuel"** (*pause*)**.**

This time, just as Eli told him to, Samuel (*pause*) **said, "Speak, Lord. I'm your servant and I'm listening."**

God gave Samuel (*pause*) **a message. He said Eli's sons were going to be punished because they didn't obey God.**

Samuel (*pause*) **went back to sleep. The next morning Eli called to him. Samuel** (*pause*) **ran to Eli and said, "Here I am."**

Eli asked what God had said to Samuel (*pause*)**. But Samuel** (*pause*) **was afraid to tell. Eli asked again, "What did God say to you? Don't hide anything from me."**

So Samuel (*pause*) **obeyed and told Eli everything God told him.**

And Eli said, "He is God. Let him do what he thinks is best."

Ask:
● **Did Samuel have to obey God and Eli?**
● **What would've happened if he hadn't obeyed?**
● **How do you think God and Eli felt about how quickly Samuel listened and obeyed?**
● **Why was Samuel quick to obey?**
● **Are you always quick to obey God and your parents? Why or why not?**

5. Choosy People

(You'll need several different snacks

such as cut-up fruit, cut-up vegetables, cheese and crackers.)

Show children the choices they have for a snack and say: **Today, you get to choose the snack you want—just like you choose whether or not to obey your parents. When we choose to obey, we learn more and we don't get hurt. But when we don't choose to obey, we may not be very happy when we get hurt or our parents discipline us. But to-day, whatever choice you make will be a good one. Let's choose our snacks.**

Allow children to choose and enjoy their snacks.

6. Pray to Obey

Close with this prayer: **Thank you, God, for people who care and teach us what's right and what's wrong. Help us choose to obey. Amen.**

by Christine Yount

NO ROOM IN THE INN

Homeless people used to be seen as hobos and bums. But not anymore. Today, families and unemployed people of all kinds have been forced to live on the streets.

Children who live in the city see homeless people almost every day on their way to school. When suburban or rural children venture into the city, homeless people can be a shocking or even frightening sight.

Use this lesson to teach children about homeless people and how to compassionately respond to them in Christ's love.

A POWERFUL PURPOSE

Children will learn about homeless people and discover compassionate ways they can reach out to the homeless.

A LOOK AT THE LESSON

1. Our Home (10 to 12 minutes)
2. A Day in the Life (10 to 12 minutes)
3. House Shopping (5 to 10 minutes)
4. Still Hungry (5 to 10 minutes)
5. One Who Cared (5 to 10 minutes)
6. Hit the Streets
7. Thank You, God (up to 5 minutes)

A SPRINKLING OF SUPPLIES

Gather an overhead projector, overhead markers, blank overhead transparencies, photocopies of the "Money Game" and "Money" handouts, scissors, playing pieces, a game die, pictures of a fancy house and an average house, tape, cardboard boxes, newspapers, canned chicken soup, bowls, spoons, napkins and a Bible.

THE LIVELY LESSON

1. Our Home

(You'll need an overhead projector, overhead markers and blank overhead transparencies. Before class, set up the overhead projector so it shines on a wall. If an overhead projector isn't available, use construction paper and markers.)

Throughout this lesson, be sensitive to needy children in your class.

Set out the overhead markers and give each child an overhead transparency. Have children draw pictures of their homes on their transparencies. As they work, go around and have them each complete the sentence, "My home is..." Write the entire sentence and the child's name at the bottom of the transparency.

Once all the transparencies are finished, collect them. Gather the children around the overhead projector. Then read the transparencies as you show each picture on the overhead projector.

Then say: **It's really nice to have homes that keep us warm in the** winter and protect us from the rain. We can thank God for our homes. But not everyone has a home. Today we're going to talk about people who don't have homes. These are people who have to live outside or in special buildings called shelters.

2. A Day in the Life

(You'll need the game board from the "Money Game" handout, play money cut from the "Money" handout, playing pieces and a game die.)

Form family teams of no more than four people. Give each family team $30 in play money and a playing piece such as a button or a coin. Gather family teams around the Money Game game board.

Explain to families that they're to begin at "start." Each family team rolls the die once and then moves its playing piece. Once the family runs out of money in the game or gets to "finish," it's out of the game. In order to ensure that at least one or two families run completely out of money, demand all the money from one or two families for taxes.

After all the family teams are out of the game, ask:
● **How did you feel as you played this game?**
● **How do you think real families feel when these things happen to them?**
● **How do you think real families feel when they don't have any money?**

3. House Shopping

(You'll need pictures of a fancy house and an average house, tape, cardboard boxes and newspapers.)

Tape the two pictures of houses to different areas of the room. Pile cardboard boxes and newspapers in another area.

Show kids the three areas where they can go shopping for a house. Tell them the fancy house will cost $10, the average house will cost $5 and the third house is free. Allow family units from the A Day in the Life activity to buy the house they can afford and sit by that house.

For the families who end up with the cardboard and newspaper house, have them build a house from their supplies and get in it.

Ask:
● **What would it be like to live in the house you got?**
● **How do you feel about the house you got? the house others got?**
● **Why did some people get better houses than others?**
● **Why do some people in real life have better houses than others?**
● **Why do some people have no houses?**

Say: **There are lots of reasons people are homeless. Some people lose all their money for the same reasons you did in the game we played. Some people abuse drugs or alcohol and can't keep a job. Others may have mental sicknesses that keep them from having a job. Let's look at how God wants us to treat people who are homeless.**

4. Still Hungry

(You'll need canned chicken soup, bowls, spoons, napkins and a Bible. Before class, prepare the soup with two or three times the amount of water the can calls for and heat it up in the church kitchen or in a Crock-Pot in your classroom. If you warm it up in your classroom, put the pot out of the way so kids can't tip it over.)

Serve children the soup and explain that this food is better than what many homeless people eat every day. As they eat, ask children to listen to what Jesus says about the homeless.

Read aloud Matthew 25:34-40 in an easy-to-understand version of the Bible or read this paraphrase: **Jesus will say to the people who obeyed him, "God is happy with you. You'll be part of God's kingdom, which he has been preparing for you since the world was made.**

"God is happy with you because you took care of me. When I was hungry, you gave me food. When I was thirsty, you gave me something to drink. When I was away from my home, you invited me into your home. When I didn't have any clothes to wear, you gave me clothes. When I was sick, you took care of me. When I was in prison, you came and visited me."

The good people asked, "Jesus, when did we do all of this for you?"

Jesus answered, "Whenever you did any of these things for anyone you met, you were really doing them for me."

Ask:

● **How does Jesus want us to treat the homeless?**

● **How do we help Jesus when we help homeless people?**

Say: **Now let's find out how one boy helped the homeless people in the city where he lived.**

5. One Who Cared

Say: **Listen to this story about a boy who helped the homeless.**

When 11-year-old Trevor Ferrell saw a news report about the homeless, he decided he could do something to help.

And he did. Trevor grabbed a blanket and a pillow. Then he convinced his family to drive 15 miles to downtown Philadelphia.

After driving around, Trevor spied a man huddled over a grate where warm air comes up from under a street. Trevor got out of the car and gave the man a soft pillow and a warm blanket. Then Trevor went home.

But the next night, Trevor and his family delivered hot food to the homeless.

Today there's a 33-room shelter named Trevor's Place. Homeless people can go there to get food and have a warm place to sleep.

"One person can make a difference," Trevor says. "Just do what you can and follow your heart."

Ask:

● **How do you think Trevor felt as he helped the homeless people?**

● **How would you feel if you had been Trevor?**

● **What are some things we can do to help the homeless?**

You may need to stimulate kids' brainstorming with these ideas: have a canned food drive to donate to a shelter, have a clothing collection to donate to a shelter, volunteer in a nearby shelter or invite a homeless person to have a meal with them.

Don't discount any of the kids' ideas. Encourage them to think big but to start small.

If you live in a town with no homeless people, encourage kids to think of ways they can help other kinds of needy people. Maybe they can collect money for an organization like Compassion International. Or they can have a canned food drive for people in their community who lose their jobs or for homeless people in a nearby town.

6. Hit the Streets

This lesson will be most effective if you can provide a hands-on situation for the children. If you know of a homeless person or family in your area, invite them to come and tell their story to your children as a closing. Talk to them before they speak to the class to make sure their comments are appropriate.

You may want to choose one of the children's ideas from the One Who Cared activity to do with the class. Or if you have a shelter or soup kitchen in your area, obtain permission from the children's parents for their children to spend time serving there after this lesson. Invite the parents to come along!

7. Thank You, God

Close with this prayer: **God, you've given so much to us. Thank you for the homes we have, the families we live with, the clothes we wear and the food we eat. Help us to remember to help people who need these things. We know that when we help them, we really help you. Amen.**

by Christine Yount

MONEY GAME

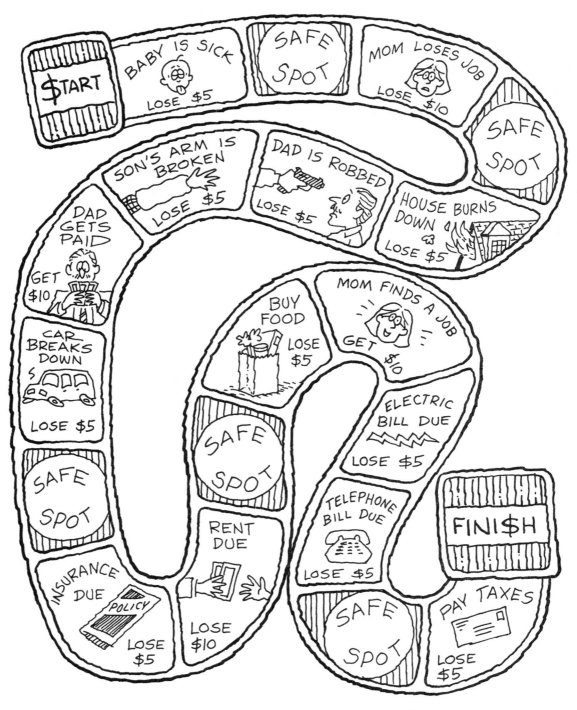

MONEY

Photocopy and cut apart enough play money for each team of four children to have $30. Make an extra photocopy to create a "bank."

PART 3:
A LIVELY LOOK
AT
CELEBRATIONS

THE BEST YEAR YET

The new year is a time for fresh starts. First- and second-graders may be struggling with behavior problems they can't shake or peer conflicts they can't resolve. They'll appreciate the chance to put things behind them and start anew.

Use this lesson to teach kids that making mistakes isn't the end of the world. God can give us a clean start whenever we mess up. This holiday can be the perfect time to teach children they can become new creations and look forward to a new beginning in Christ.

THE POWERFUL PURPOSE

Children will learn to begin the new year as a new creation in Christ.

A LOOK AT THE LESSON

1. Last Year's Events (5 to 10 minutes)
2. A Time for Everything (up to 5 minutes)
3. Clean-Start Journals (5 to 10 minutes)
4. Party Hats (5 to 10 minutes)
5. Party Time (up to 5 minutes)
6. Party Treats (up to 5 minutes)
7. A New Year's Prayer (up to 5 minutes)

A SPRINKLING OF SUPPLIES

Gather masking tape, newsprint, markers or crayons, a Bible, construc-tion paper, white paper, a hole punch, ribbon or yarn, scissors, 9×12-inch paper, balloons, cookies and punch.

THE LIVELY LESSON

1. Last Year's Events

(You'll need masking tape, news-print and markers or crayons.)

Tape several sheets of newsprint to the wall with the edges overlapping slightly to make a large mural. Write on the top "What I did last year..."

Distribute markers or crayons. Have children draw pictures or write words on the mural to show what they've done in the last year. You may need to give them a reference point such as "Think about what you've done since last Christmas." If kids still have diffi-culty, ask them if they've taken field trips or vacations, or if anything spe-cial has happened in their family such as the birth of a new brother or sister.

Encourage the children to make several drawings and to tell the chil-dren working on either side of them about their drawings.

When children finish their drawings and have told their neighbors about the drawings, say: **We're celebrating New Year's Day today. On New Year's Day the year 19__ ends, and the year 19__ begins. We can look forward to lots of brand new ad-ventures that will happen in the year ahead.**

2. A Time for Everything

(You'll need an easy-to-understand translation of the Bible.)

Have kids spread out throughout the room and stand with arms extended. Tell them to twirl around once to make an imaginary circle that doesn't touch anyone else's circle. Tell the children they can act these verses out in any way they want, but they can't touch anyone and they have to stay inside their circle.

Open your Bible to Ecclesiastes 3:3b-8. Read the passage and pause after each phrase while kids act it out.

Afterward, have children gather together and sit down on the floor.

Ask:

● **Have you ever done something you're really proud of? Explain.** Encourage children's responses.

Ask:

● **How does it feel to be proud of something you've done?**

● **Have you ever done something you wish you hadn't done? Explain.** Encourage children's responses. Be sensitive to hurting children.

Ask:

● **How do you feel when you do something you shouldn't?**

Say: **The Bible says that good things happen and bad things happen. The good news is that we can wipe away the bad things and start all over again. New Year's is a good time to start over again because it's a brand new year.**

3. Clean-Start Journals

(You'll need construction paper, crayons or markers, white paper, a hole punch and ribbon or yarn.)

Say: **When we become Christians, God makes us brand new. The Bible says that all the bad things we do are wiped away, and we are shiny and clean. We can start all over again.**

This is a good time to explain your church or denomination's thoughts on how people become Christians.

Give each child a sheet of construction paper and crayons or markers. Have them fold it in half widthwise and write along the bottom this paraphrase of Revelation 21:5, "God says, 'I make all things

CLEAN-START JOURNALS

new.'" Write the words on a piece of paper or on a chalkboard to help kids with spelling. You may need to help beginning readers. Have the children decorate their construction paper covers with the crayons or markers. Then have kids join you in reading the paraphrase aloud.

Give each child several sheets of white paper and say: **This paper is clean and empty, just like the new year is clean and empty. Nothing bad has happened yet. You can choose how you fill up your paper and you can choose how you'll behave in the new year. You can fill up the year with good, kind and loving things or you can fill it up with not-so-good things.**

Have the children fold their white paper in half widthwise and put it inside the construction paper cover. Punch two holes near the folded edge of the paper and tie the papers together with ribbon or yarn to make a journal.

Tell the children to take their journals home. Tell them to draw pictures, paste magazine pictures or write a story each time something happens in the new year that they want to remember. Tell them to fill up a page each time they choose to do something that makes God happy. At the end of the year they can look back through their journals to remember all the fun things they did, and they'll be able to see how they've made choices to follow God.

4. Party Hats

(You'll need scissors, 9×12-inch paper, crayons or markers, tape and yarn.)

PARTY HATS

For each child in your class, cut out a half-circle from a 9×12-inch sheet of paper. Give half-circles and crayons or markers to children.

Say: **At New Year's, people make resolutions. A resolution can be a promise to do a good thing or a promise not to do a bad thing. Think of a promise you'd like to make for the new year and draw a picture about it on your piece of paper.**

Tell kids not to color too close to the straight edges. If they do, when the circles are folded, part of their picture will be covered up. When kids are finished, have them tell one other person about their resolution. Then help them fold and tape the circles to make hats. Tape 12-inch lengths of yarn to the inside of the hats to make chin straps.

5. Party Time

(You'll need inflated balloons and the party hats.)

Say: **On New Year's Eve, people have parties to count down the time to the new year. Let's have our own party and celebrate being brand new creations in Jesus.**

Have children put on their party hats. Spread the balloons out on the floor. There should be enough balloons for each child to have at least one to pop.

Have kids count down from 10 to zero with you. On zero, have everyone yell, "Happy New Year. God makes us brand new." Then have the kids race to pop all the balloons.

6. Party Treats

(You'll need a party treat such as cookies and punch.)

Serve the cookies and punch. Ask children what their favorite memory from last year is. Then ask children to guess what will happen in the new year.

7. A New Year's Prayer

Close in prayer, thanking God for clean beginnings. Thank him for making us new creatures and for taking away the bad things we've done. Also ask for help in keeping resolutions.

by Janel Kauffman

HERE'S MY HEART

For most people, Valentine's Day is a day to acknowledge sweethearts and loved ones. But if we focus on God's love, Valentine's Day can be like Christmas and Easter all rolled into one. We can celebrate God's love in his sending Jesus, Jesus' sacrifice on the cross and our commitment to love others.

Use this lesson to teach children that God loves them and to show them how to love God.

A POWERFUL PURPOSE

Children will learn that God loves them, and they'll learn to show their love for God.

A LOOK AT THE LESSON

1. Find a Valentine (8 to 10 minutes)
2. God Is Love (5 minutes)
3. His Love in Us (5 to 10 minutes)
4. Love Reflection (5 to 10 minutes)
5. Celebrate Love (5 to 10 minutes)
6. Love Feast (up to 5 minutes)
7. We Love God (up to 5 minutes)
8. Songfest (up to 5 minutes)

A SPRINKLING OF SUPPLIES

You'll need photocopies of the "Heart Squares" handout on red paper. Gather scissors, a Bible, markers, cardboard, tape, Popsicle sticks, aluminum foil, red and pink paper, glitter, paper doilies, glue, party decorations, a cassette of praise music, a cassette player, iced cupcakes, red punch, paper cups, napkins and small candies.

THE LIVELY LESSON

1. Find a Valentine

(Before class, make enough photocopies of the "Heart Squares" handout on red paper for each child to have 20 heart squares. Cut apart the heart squares and hide them throughout the room.)

Form teams of two to four kids. Pick one child in each team to be the valentine-keeper. All other team members are valentine-givers.

Tell kids there are valentines hidden all over the room. The team that finds the most valentines at the end of five minutes wins. Here are the rules:

● The valentine-givers can only deliver one valentine at a time to the valentine-keeper.

● As the valentine-givers deliver each valentine, they must say, "Here's a pretty valentine for you."

● As the valentine-keepers receive a valentine, they must say, "Thank you for the pretty valentine."

● The valentine-keepers must sit still during the game. They can cheer for the valentine-givers, but they can't move or help in any way.

Call time after the five minutes are up and have each team count their valentines. Declare a winner.

Ask:

● **Which do you like best—giving**

valentines or getting valentines?

● **What's fun about giving valentines?**

● **What's fun about getting valentines?**

Say: **It's fun to get valentines from people who care about us, and it's also fun to give valentines to show others we care for them. Let's find out about God's valentine for us.**

2. God Is Love

(You'll need the heart squares kids found during the Find a Valentine activity, a Bible and markers. Have extra heart squares available in case some teams didn't find many in the last activity.)

Have all the kids sit in a circle. Have the valentine-keepers give handfuls of the heart squares to the others in the circle.

Ask:

● **How do you know when someone loves you?**

Say: **The Bible tells us God loves each of us.** Read 1 John 4:9 in a translation that's easy for kids to understand.

Ask:

● **What did Jesus do when he was on the earth that showed he loved people?**

Say: **Jesus came to earth because God loves you. Write your name on one of these valentines to show that God has sent Jesus as a special valentine to you.**

Distribute markers. Have each child write his or her name on one of the heart squares and put the square in a pile in the middle of the circle. Then have them think of other people they know who God loves. Each time they

think of someone, have them put another heart square onto the pile.

Say: **Look at all the hearts in this pile. God loves everyone and his valentine to us is Jesus. But God's love doesn't stop there. God has something important for each of us to do.**

3. His Love in Us

(You'll need a Bible.)

Say: **Jesus doesn't live on earth anymore, so God made us his messengers of love.**

Read 1 John 4:11-12, 19-21 in an easy-to-understand translation.

Ask:

● **How can we show people that we love them?**

Have kids find partners. Assign each pair someone they can show love to, such as a parent, a brother, a sister, a grandparent, a neighbor or a teacher. Give pairs several minutes to think of ways they can show love to those people. Then gather the children in a circle, and have each pair pantomime how they would love that person. Let the other children guess what they're doing.

Say: **You have great ideas on how to love people. When you show others you love them, you're also showing them God loves them.**

4. Love Reflection

(Before class, cut enough 6-inch cardboard squares for each child to have one. You'll also need tape, Popsicle sticks, aluminum foil, red and pink paper, glitter, paper doilies, glue and markers.)

Pass out the cardboard squares. Have kids tape a Popsicle stick to the back of the square to act as a handle.

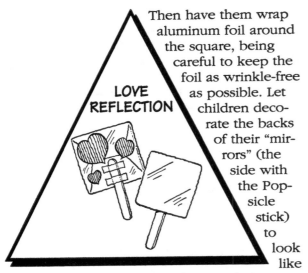

Then have them wrap aluminum foil around the square, being careful to keep the foil as wrinkle-free as possible. Let children decorate the backs of their "mirrors" (the side with the Popsicle stick) to look like valentines. Have kids write their names on the backs of the Popsicle sticks. Set the mirrors aside to dry.

5. Celebrate Love

(You'll need party decorations, a cassette of praise music and a cassette player.)

Say: **Let's throw a party to show our love for God and each other.** Bring out the party decorations and play the music. Have kids decorate the room for a party.

6. Love Feast

(You'll need the cassette of praise music and cassette player, iced cupcakes, red punch, paper cups, napkins and small candies such as chocolate chips, red hots and rainbow sprinkles.)

Continue playing the praise music. Have kids find partners. Have children find out what their partners want on their cupcakes. Then have them prepare the cupcakes according to their partners' preferences.

Say: **One way we show our love for each other is to do kind things for each other. Another way is to compliment each other. As you eat your snack, tell your partner one thing you like about him or her.**

7. We Love God

(You'll need the mirrors the children made in the Love Reflection activity.)

If the day is sunny, have kids put on their coats and go outside for this activity. If the day is cloudy, this activity can be done with available classroom light.

Gather kids in a circle. Have kids hold their mirrors so they reflect the sunlight upward. Say: **God loves us all the time. We can reflect God's love back to him when we spend time with him.**

Then have kids reflect the sunlight onto each other. Tell them not to shine the sunlight in each other's eyes. Say: **We show God's love to others when we do kind and loving things for each other.**

8. Songfest

Lead children in singing the song "This Is My Commandment." You can find it in *The Group Songbook* (Group Books).

Pray: **Thank you, God, for loving us so much you sent your son. Help us reflect your love to all the people we meet. Amen.**

HEART SQUARES

Make enough photocopies of this handout so that every child will have 20 heart squares. Cut apart the squares and hide them around the room before class.

CREATION CELEBRATION

Children hear about the importance of saving the planet at school, on television and on radio. But the best reason for saving the planet is rarely acknowledged by the mainstream media. Children need to learn that we should take care of the earth because God created us to be caretakers.

Use this lesson to give kids a Christian foundation for celebrating Earth Day.

A POWERFUL PURPOSE

Children will learn to take care of Earth because it belongs to God.

A LOOK AT THE LESSON

1. Creation Re-creation (5 to 10 minutes)
2. Puff-Ball Creations (5 to 10 minutes)
3. Creature Care (up to 5 minutes)
4. Everything Counts (5 to 10 minutes)
5. What to Do? (up to 5 minutes)
6. Nature Snacks (up to 5 minutes)
7. We Can Do It (5 to 10 minutes)
8. Help Us, God (up to 5 minutes)

A SPRINKLING OF SUPPLIES

Gather a Bible, a flashlight, dirt, a spray bottle filled with water, a plant, craft pompoms, construction paper, pipe cleaners, glue, scissors, egg cartons, string or yarn, fruit, cups, napkins, newsprint, markers, a stapler and blunt-end scissors.

THE LIVELY LESSON

1. Creation Re-creation

(You'll need a Bible, a flashlight, dirt in a small bag, a spray bottle filled with water and a plant.)

Gather children in an open area and sit down in a circle. Tell this story of creation, using the props as indicated.

Open the Bible to Genesis 1. Say: **In the very beginning, before there was anything, God decided to create the universe. So God made light** (turn on the flashlight). **He separated the light from the darkness** (turn off the flashlight) **and called the light "daytime" and the darkness "nighttime"** (turn the flashlight on and off as you say day and night). **He made all of this on the first day.**

Then God made air (have kids blow air as though they were blowing out a candle). **He made the sky** (have kids point to the sky). **He did all of this on the second day.**

Next God gathered all the water (Mist water into the air. Don't drench any of the children, but it's okay if they get a little wet.) **and made it separate from the dry land. He called the dry land "earth"** (pass around the dirt) **and he called the water "seas." He made plants grow** (pass around the plant). **All of this happened on the third day.**

Then God made more light *(turn on the flashlight and pass it around the circle).* **He made the sun for the daytime and the moon and stars for the nighttime. He hung them all in the sky. All of these were made on the fourth day.**

Then God made birds and fish *(have kids flap their arms like wings and make fish faces).* **They were made on the fifth day.**

Next God made all the animals *(have kids make animal sounds).* **He also made humans** *(have kids point to each other).* **He made man to be like God and take care of all the things God had created. God looked at all the things he created and they were all good. This was the sixth day.**

On the seventh day, everything was finished so God rested.

2. Puff-Ball Creations

(You'll need craft pompoms, construction paper, pipe cleaners, glue, scissors and egg cartons.)

Say: **Let's make some creations of our own to see how God felt when he made the world.**

Have children make creatures out of the pompoms, construction paper, pipe cleaners and glue. They can look like real creatures or they can be made-up creatures. Have the kids decide what their creations can do and name them. Have each child make several. Cut apart egg cartons so each child has just the right number of cups for his or her creatures. Then have the kids put their creations in egg cups. The egg cartons are the "habitat" of the creatures. Explain to the children that a creature's habitat is the world or home where it lives. Have children

decide what their habitat is like. For example, if a child made all sea creatures, his or her habitat may be cold and wet.

Ask:

● **How does it feel to create a world?**

● **What will your creatures need in order to live?**

3. Creature Care

(You'll need the creatures and habitats.)

Have the children find partners and explain their creatures and their habitats to each other.

Say: **You won't be taking care of the world you made. Your partner will keep it from now on. You'll have to trust that your partner knows how to take care of your creatures so they'll live a good life.**

Then have them exchange creatures and habitats.

Ask:

● **What do you need to tell your partner so he or she will know how to take care of your world?**

● **How do you feel about giving up your world to someone else?**

● **What'll you do if your partner doesn't take care of your world?**

Say: **God has given us his world to take care of just like you've given your world to your partner to take care of. It makes God sad when he sees us hurting the world we live in instead of taking care of it. We need to remember to do everything we can to take care of the world because God is counting on us.**

4. Everything Counts

(You'll need two 10-foot pieces of string or yarn.)

In an open area of the room, make a circle with the string. This will be Lake Beautiful. Attach one end of the other piece of string to the lake and stretch it out. This will be the peaceful stream.

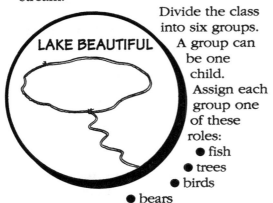

Divide the class into six groups. A group can be one child. Assign each group one of these roles:

● fish
● trees
● birds
● bears
● berry bushes
● people

Tell this story and pause to let each group act out its role. Say: **Lake Beautiful was a peaceful place. There were tall trees close by the water** (pause). **The birds made nests in the trees and took care of their babies** (pause). **Fish swam in the water** (pause). **And bears ate berries from the berry bushes and fish from the lake** (pause). **People came from all over to have picnics at Lake Beautiful** (pause).

The people decided they wanted to build a cabin, so they cut down all the trees (pause). **They didn't leave any trees and they didn't plant any new trees. The birds had no place to live and raise their babies. All the birds flew away** (pause).

Then the people started to dump all their trash into the lake (pause). **Soon the lake got so dirty with all the trash that the fish couldn't live there anymore. So they all traveled down the stream to find another lake** (pause). **The bears couldn't eat fish anymore and had to eat berries all the time** (pause). **But there weren't enough berries to feed all the bears so the bears had to move away** (pause).

The people looked at their beautiful spot and realized that it wasn't beautiful anymore. So they moved away, too (pause).

Gather children and ask:

● **How did the people's actions affect all the animals?**

5. What to Do?

(You'll need the string lake and stream.)

Ask:

● **What happened to Lake Beautiful?**

● **What could the people do to make Lake Beautiful a pretty place again?**

Have kids assume their roles again to act out their ideas for cleaning up Lake Beautiful. They may plant new trees or have a diving expedition to clean the trash out of the lake. Encourage creative responses to clean up Lake Beautiful.

Gather kids again and say: **You've made Lake Beautiful a pretty place again and the bears, birds and fish can move back.**

Ask:

● **What should the people do to keep Lake Beautiful from getting dirty again?**

Have kids assume their roles one more time to act out ideas for keeping the lake beautiful. They might mention recycling, planting new trees or feeding the birds.

Gather the children and ask:

● **What do you already do at**

home, at school or at church to make our world a pretty place?

● **What else could we do?**

You may want to start a class recycling project. Provide boxes in your class where kids can put paper scraps or bring in cans to recycle. Give any money you make to charity. You may want to have a water monitor who would make sure no one in class wastes water or a stuff monitor who would make sure no one throws away anything that can be reused or recycled.

6. Nature Snacks

(You'll need cut-up fruit, water, reusable cups and napkins.)

Serve natural treats such as apples, oranges, carrot sticks or celery sticks. Enjoy the treats with cold water. As you eat, have each child talk about his or her favorite part of God's creation.

7. We Can Do It

(You'll need newsprint, markers, construction paper, a stapler and blunt-end scissors.)

Use newsprint to make a mural or cover a bulletin board. With a marker write "We Can Take Care of God's World" at the top of the mural. Read the words to the children.

Distribute construction paper. Have children tear out the shape of some part of God's creation. Have them decorate their shapes with the markers. Staple the creations to the mural where children want their shapes to appear.

Distribute more of construction paper and blunt-end scissors. Have them each trace their hand on the construction paper, and then cut out the hand shape. Staple the paper hands to the mural where children want them.

Say: **Each of you can use your hands to take care of God's creation.**

8. Help Us, God

Close in prayer, thanking God for all the beautiful things he's created and asking for help to take care of the world.

by Maureen Hollen

BACK TO SCHOOL

Though they may be reluctant to admit it, children going into the first and second grade often have very real fears. They worry about having a new teacher and learning a new routine and they worry that the schoolwork may be too difficult.

Kids need to learn that a new school year is a time to celebrate new opportunities. God is powerful enough to help them through any new and scary situation. They can depend on him and look forward to a new year.

A POWERFUL PURPOSE

Children will learn that a new school year is an opportunity for fun and growth and that God will help them conquer their fears.

A LOOK AT THE LESSON

1. We're Going to School (up to 5 minutes)
2. School Song (up to 5 minutes)
3. "Boo!" Tag (5 to 10 minutes)
4. Moses Was Scared (5 to 10 minutes)
5. Depending on God (up to 5 minutes)
6. A School Treat (up to 5 minutes)
7. God Goes to School (up to 5 minutes)
8. Let's Pray (up to 5 minutes)

A SPRINKLING OF SUPPLIES

Gather a Bible, happy face or star stickers, vanilla wafers, milk, paper cups, napkins, colored chalk and sandpaper.

THE LIVELY LESSON

1. We're Going to School

(Before class, set up chairs in rows of four with an aisle between the middle chairs. These will serve as the seats on a school bus. Put one chair at the front of the rows on the left to be the driver's seat.)

As kids arrive, say: **We're going to school today.** Have them find seats on the school bus.

When everyone has found a seat on the bus, board the bus, sit in the driver's seat and drive the kids to school. Have the kids make driving noises. Have them lean and make squealing tire noises when you round the corners. Pull up in front of the school.

Before letting the kids off the bus, ask:

● **What do you like about school?**
● **What don't you like about school?**
● **What's fun about starting a new year of school?**
● **What's scary about starting a new year of school?**

Say: **Going back to school is exciting, but it can be scary, too. Today we're going to talk about what you can do when you're scared.**

2. School Song

(Before class, put a small table in

the front to act as a teachers desk. Put a chalkboard or an erasable marker-board at the front. Write simple math equations and simple words on the board.)

Have children file out of the bus and line up beside it.

Sing the words below to the tune of "Heigh Ho" from the Walt Disney movie *Snow White*. Lead the kids around the room as you sing this song several times.

> **To learn, to learn,**
> **I go to school to learn**
> **About reading and math and**
> **science and art,**
> **To learn, to learn, to learn.**

Lead children to an area set up like a schoolroom. Have children sit on the floor facing the chalkboard or marker-board.

3. "Boo!" Tag

Ask:

● **What are some things that scare kids about going back to school?**

● **What do you do when you're scared?**

Say: **Let's pretend it's recess and play a game about fears.**

If possible, take kids outside for this lively game. Choose a volunteer to be the "Super Student." Everyone else is a "fear." The fears can taunt the Super Student, but the fears must freeze in place when the Super Student tags them and says "Boo!" The last fear to be frozen becomes the new Super Student. Play several times.

Say: **It's fun to freeze our fears in a game, but sometimes it's harder to stop being scared. Let's find out what a man in the Bible did when he was scared.**

4. Moses Was Scared

(You'll need a Bible.)

Open the Bible to Exodus 3–4. Tell kids to listen closely to the story. Every time you say the words "scared" and "afraid," they should cover their eyes with their hands as though they were afraid.

Say: **One day, Moses was taking care of his father-in-law's sheep. He made sure they had plenty to eat and drink, and he protected them from animals that would eat the sheep.**

As he led the flock, he noticed a bush that was on fire. But the bush didn't burn up. Moses decided he needed a closer look so he walked closer to the bush.

Then God called, "Moses, Moses!"

Moses said, "Here I am."

Then God said, "Don't come any closer. Take off your sandals because you're standing on holy ground."

Moses did what God said and covered his face because he was afraid to look at God.

God said, "I have a special job for you. My people are suffering in Egypt. I want you to tell the king of Egypt to let my people leave."

Moses was scared. He'd never done anything like this before. He said, "I'm not very important. I wouldn't even know what to say. How can I do this?"

God said, "I'll be with you the whole time. Don't worry."

God told Moses exactly what to say, but Moses was still scared. So God gave him miracles to perform to prove to the people that God really had sent Moses.

When Moses threw his walking

stick on the ground, it turned into a snake. When he picked it up again, it turned back into a walking stick.

When Moses put his hand into his coat and pulled it out, it had a terrible disease. When he put his hand into his coat and pulled it out again, it was healthy.

God said, "If the people still don't believe you, take some water from the river. When you pour it on the ground, it'll turn into blood."

Even with the miracles, Moses was still scared. He said, "I'm not very good at speaking, God. Please send someone else."

God said, "I will teach you what to say. But since you're still scared, I'll send your brother Aaron with you. He'll help you."

Moses did what God said. He was still a little bit scared, but he knew God would take care of him. Moses went to the king and told him to let God's people leave. It took a long time, but with God's help, Moses convinced the king to let the people leave.

Finally, God's people left Egypt. With God's help, Moses led them to the land that God promised them, and they made a new country called Israel.

5. Depending on God

(You'll need happy face or star stickers.)

Say: **The Bible says God will never leave us alone. He's always watching us to make sure we're safe. We can depend on God to always take care of us.**

Give children each a sticker, and tell them to put it on the corner of their school desk, on their lunch box or on a notebook. Tell them it's a reminder that God is always there beside them to take care of them.

Say: **Every time you get worried or scared, look at the sticker and remember God loves you and is there to help you.**

6. A School Treat

(You'll need vanilla wafers, milk, paper cups and napkins.)

Serve the snack. As children eat, have them each tell what their favorite part of school is and what their least favorite part of school is. Have them tell you what they think they'll learn in the new school year.

7. God Goes to School

(You'll need colored chalk and sheets of fine sandpaper.)

Say: **God is always with you, even when you're scared. He even goes to school with you. He'll take care of you. Let's make pictures that show how God will take care of you at school.**

Distribute chalk and sheets of sandpaper. When children finish their pictures, have them tell the people on both sides of them how God will take care of them in school.

8. Let's Pray

Close with this prayer: **God, you are big enough to take care of all of us. You're with us even when we're scared. Help us learn to depend on you so we can learn and have fun in school. Amen.**

BIBLE HEROES

First- and second-graders look up to all kinds of heroes, especially the Saturday-morning fantasy kind whose powers children could never hope to imitate. Children need to see that real heroes are ordinary people who have the courage to obey an extraordinary God.

This lesson can be used before All Saints' Day or Halloween to encourage children to follow God boldly, realizing that all the power in the universe is behind them.

A POWERFUL PURPOSE

Children will learn that true heroes are ordinary people who are willing to obey God.

A LOOK AT THE LESSON

1. Parade of Heroes (10 to 12 minutes)
2. Bible Hall of Fame (5 to 10 minutes)
3. A Brave Queen (up to 5 minutes)
4. Trust Me? (up to 5 minutes)
5. Blue-Ribbon Heroes (up to 5 minutes)
6. Hero Food (up to 5 minutes)
7. Heroes' Prayer (up to 5 minutes)

A SPRINKLING OF SUPPLIES

Gather Bible costume items such as bathrobes, towels and strips of cloth. You'll also need Bible storybooks, a Bible, 3x5 cards, scissors, markers, blue ribbon cut in 10-inch strips, a stapler, tape, safety pins, graham crackers, honey in squeeze bottles and wet washcloths.

THE LIVELY LESSON

1. Parade of Heroes

(You'll need bathrobes, towels and strips of cloth for Bible costumes. If you can arrange to borrow costumes used in Christmas and Easter pageants, children will be thrilled to wear them.)

As children arrive, show them the costume materials. Invite children to dress up as their favorite Bible characters. They may choose to dress up as Peter, Paul, David, Moses, Mary, Joseph or Esther. Encourage kids to work together to assemble and put on their costumes. Affirm the cooperative efforts you see.

When all the children are costumed, teach them this marching song to the tune of "The Farmer in the Dell."

A hero's what I am,
A hero's what I am,
Trusting God in all I do,
A hero's what I am.

Have the children sing as they march around the room. Then gather everyone in a circle, and invite kids each to tell which Bible hero their costume represents. It's okay if not all the children can name a specific person from the Bible.

Ask:

● **What's fun about dressing up as someone else?**

● **What's a hero?**

It's okay if kids mention super-natural qualities or heroes such as Teenage Mutant Ninja Turtles. At this point, don't correct them by saying, "But that's not what God says a hero is." Use this activity to get children thinking about what a hero is. The rest of the lesson will teach what God's idea of a hero is.

Ask:

● **Do you think you could ever be a hero? Why or why not?**

Say: **Today we're going to talk about heroes from the Bible. I think you're going to find out some surprising things.**

2. Bible Hall of Fame

(You'll need several Bible story-books. Look in your church library or at a Christian bookstore to find books on people such as Daniel, Samuel, Dorcas and Lydia. Set the books out on a table where children can look through them.)

Say: **Today I'm going to give you a chance to be the teacher! Look through these books until you find one about your favorite Bible hero. Then everyone who wants to can take a turn telling about his or her favorite Bible hero.**

Encourage children to share the books. Some children will need help reading the books. Keep the presentations brief by asking questions to move things along such as "What did David do that made him a hero?" Let more than one child contribute to each story.

Say: **Now we're going to have fun with a story about one of my favor-ite Bible heroes—a brave queen.**

3. A Brave Queen

(You'll need a Bible.)

Tell the girls to pop up and down every time you say "queen" or "Esther." Have the boys pop up and down each time you say "king."

Open the Bible to the book of Esther. Say: **Once a long time ago, King Xerxes** (pronounced Zerk-sees) **of Persia decided to search for a queen. Many beautiful young women were brought to the king, and out of them all he chose a love-ly Jewish girl named Esther to be his queen.**

One day a wicked man named Haman got angry at Queen Esther's uncle. Haman tricked King Xerxes into signing a law that said all Jews were to be destroyed.

When Queen Esther heard about the law, she asked all the Jews to pray for her. So they did—for three days and nights. Then Esther went to see the king. Now this was a very dangerous thing to do because any-one who went to see the king with-out special permission could be killed.

When the king saw Esther com-ing, he held out his gold staff to welcome her. She was safe!

Esther invited the king and Haman to two special dinners. At the second dinner the king asked Esther, "What do you want from me? Whatever you ask, I'll do for you."

Esther answered, "Please, save my life and the lives of my people. A wicked man has ordered us to be put to death!"

King Xerxes asked, "Who would do such a thing?"

Esther answered, "Haman!"

That very day Haman was killed. The king issued a new order for the Jews to protect themselves from all their enemies. The Jews all got to-

gether and had a big party to celebrate. To this very day, the Jewish
people remember brave Queen
Esther who trusted God and saved
her people!

Ask:

● **What did Queen Esther do that
made her a hero?**

4. Trust Me?

Say: **Esther was just an ordinary
person. She didn't have any magical
powers. But she did have something special that you can have, too.**

Ask:

● **Can you guess what it is?**

Say: **Esther trusted in God. She
knew he'd take care of her and her
people. The Bible says to be strong
in the Lord and in his great power**
(Ephesians 6:10). **Being strong in the
Lord doesn't mean we need great
big muscles. It means we need to
trust in our great big God! Let's see
what it feels like to trust.**

Have children form a line facing
one wall of the classroom.

Walk behind the line and say: **Close
your eyes and keep them shut. No
fair peeking at all! Hold your arms
straight down at your sides. When I
say your name, keep your body
stiff and fall backward.**

Stand about 18 inches behind a
child, call the child's name, then catch
the child as he or she falls backward
toward you. After you've caught all the
students, gather everyone in an open
area and sit down.

Ask:

● **How did you feel when I called
your name?**

● **How did you feel after I caught
you?**

● **How are those feelings like the**

way Esther might've felt?

Say: **Just now you obeyed and
trusted me, even when it was a little scary. Esther obeyed and trusted
God in a scary situation. That's
what made her a hero. When you
obey and trust God, you can be
heroes, too!**

If any of the children didn't fall
backward and let you catch them, use
the teachable moment to talk about
how hard it is to trust God. Ask questions like "Why was it hard to trust
me?" and "How was trying to trust me
like trying to trust God?" Then say,
"Trusting God is hard, but when we
do, God always takes care of us."

5. Blue-Ribbon Heroes

(You'll need 3×5 cards, scissors,
markers, blue ribbon cut in 10-inch
strips, a stapler, tape and safety pins.
Cut the 3×5 cards in half.)

Give each child half a card, a marker
and a length of blue ribbon. Help children write "Trust God" on their cards.
Then help them fold their ribbons in
half and staple them to their cards.
Tape safety pins on the backs of the

HERO
RIBBONS

cards and pin them on the children.

Say: **Now you're official blue-ribbon heroes. Remember to keep trusting in God!**

6. Hero Food

(You'll need graham crackers and honey in squeeze bottles. Have warm, wet washcloths available to clean sticky hands.)

Tell kids that even heroes need a good healthy snack and that they've earned some hero food. Distribute crackers and have kids take turns squeezing honey onto their crackers. Explain that honey was a favorite treat in Bible times.

7. Heroes' Prayer

When children have finished their snacks, gather them in a circle and hold hands. In a closing prayer, thank God for protecting them and pray that each child will keep trusting in God.

by Lois Keffer

HARVEST CELEBRATION

In nearly every culture, harvest is a time to celebrate. And kids love a celebration! But most children are removed from the agricultural process. To most children, apples, tomatoes and green beans come from the store, not from carefully tended gardens that rely on God's rich soil, sunshine and rain.

Use this lesson to teach children that all good things come from God and that it's pleasing to God when we celebrate his bounty.

A POWERFUL PURPOSE

Children will recognize God as the giver of the good things they enjoy and understand that God appreciates their thanks and praise.

A LOOK AT THE LESSON

1. Popcorn Blowout (5 to 10 minutes)
2. Alphabet Pop-Up Praises (5 to 10 minutes)
3. Leaf Rubbings (5 to 10 minutes)
4. Thank You Tree (5 to 10 minutes)
5. Psalm in Motion (up to 5 minutes)
6. Circle of Friendship (up to 5 minutes)

A SPRINKLING OF SUPPLIES

Gather a tablecloth, a hot-air popcorn popper, an extension cord, unpopped popcorn, leaves, newsprint, crayons, tape, construction paper, scissors, markers and a Bible.

THE LIVELY LESSON

1. Popcorn Blowout

(You'll need a large plastic tablecloth, a hot-air popcorn popper, an extension cord and unpopped popcorn. Spread the tablecloth on the floor in the center of the room. Pour popcorn into popper and place it in the center of the tablecloth with the lid off.)

As children arrive, invite them to sit around the edge of the tablecloth. Turn the popcorn popper on. Seat yourself beside the power cord to prevent children from handling it. As the popcorn heats up, ask children if they like popcorn, when they usually eat it and if they've ever made or eaten popcorn balls.

When the popcorn shoots out of the popper, invite kids to help themselves. They'll have a giggling good time catching it in the air and gathering it from the tablecloth. Make sure kids don't get close enough to the popper to touch it. It's hot enough to burn.

When the popcorn feast is finished, ask:

● **What was it like to catch and gobble up the popcorn?**

● **Where do all the good things we have to eat come from?**

Say: **God gives us all kinds of good things to eat. That's one way God shows his love for us. When we see how much God loves us, we want to love him right back. That's**

what we're going to do next.

Have the children help you quickly put away the popcorn popper and the tablecloth and pick up any leftover popcorn.

2. Alphabet Pop-Up Praises

Gather children in an open area of the room and have them squat down.

Say: **Now you get a chance to *be* the popcorn! I'm going to say a letter of the alphabet. If you can think of something you're thankful for that starts with that letter, pop up and say it. For example, if I say "A," what could you pop up and say?**

Just remember, not all the popcorn popped at one time. That would make a big explosion! You'll need to take turns popping up, just as the popcorn did. Here we go!

Children may have trouble naming things that begin with some letters. In that case, pop up and name something yourself or go on to the next letter.

When you reach the last letter, say: **You were wonderful popcorn!**

Ask:

● **How did it feel to give "popcorn praises"?**

● **How do you feel when someone thanks you for doing something?**

● **How do you think God feels when he hears all the things we're thankful for?**

Say: **It feels good when people tell us they appreciate the things we do for them. God has those kinds of feelings, too. Even though God is great and powerful, he likes to hear us say thank you.**

3. Leaf Rubbings

(You'll need several samples of many different kinds of leaves. Or,

take children on a walk to gather their own leaves. You'll also need large sheets of newsprint and crayons.)

Show children how to press a leaf under a sheet of newsprint, then rub over the newsprint lightly with crayon. Encourage children to experiment with color and to create designs using several leaves.

Ask:

● **What do you like about leaves?**

● **If you could be a tree, what kind of tree would you be?**

● **Why do you think God gave us trees and leaves?**

Say: **Let's all stretch as tall as we can and pretend our arms are branches and wave our branches to the sky and say, "Thank you, God, for giving us trees!"**

Ask:

● **What else has God made that we can be thankful for?**

Have children come up with actions to say thank you to God for each thing they mention.

4. Thank You Tree

(You'll need tape, newsprint, a brown crayon, construction paper, scissors and markers. Before class, tape sheets of newsprint together on a wall. With a brown crayon, quickly sketch a large tree with bare branches. Cut simple leaf shapes from construction paper.)

Ask:

● **When do you bring a tree inside your house?**

● **How does it feel to decorate a Christmas tree?**

Say: **Today we're going to decorate a different kind of tree—a "thank you" tree.**

Ask:

● **What kinds of things do you**

think we should put on our thank you tree?

Draw a stick figure of a child on a construction paper leaf. Say: **I'm thankful for all of you, so I'm putting this picture of a child on the thank you tree. This is my way of saying, "Thank you, God, for these children."**

Have children draw pictures of what they're thankful for on leaves. Then tape the leaves to the tree. Have each child make several leaves.

After the tree is decorated, ask:

● **How did you feel as you decorated this thank you tree?**

● **Does our tree make God happy?**

Say: **All these wonderful things you put on the tree come from God. God wants us to enjoy all of them. And he wants us to remember to say thank you.**

5. Psalm in Motion

(You'll need a Bible.)

Read Psalm 65:9-13 from an easy-to-understand version of the Bible. Invite children to make up motions to go with each verse. For example, as you read verse 9, children might pretend they're watering a field, then wiggle their fingers and reach up high to represent growing grain.

Go through the psalm two or three times so children can rehearse and refine their motions. Have a good time shouting and singing for joy at the close of the psalm!

You may want to perform this psalm in a church service.

6. Circle of Friendship

Gather children in a circle. Have them extend their hands forward, palms up, as you pray: **God, thank you for all the good things you've given us, like** (name things the children gave thanks for during the lesson). **You've made us very happy, and we want to make you happy by saying thank you. Amen.**

by Lois Keffer

Noel, Noel!

Christmas is an exciting—and stressful—time of year for children. Families frantically race from shopping malls to parties to Christmas pageants. And somewhere in all the bustle of cookie baking, present wrapping and happy anticipation of what will appear under the tree, the spirit of giving is often lost.

This lesson will help children experience the wonder and joy of Christmas and help them realize they have a lot to give.

A POWERFUL PURPOSE

Children will celebrate God's gift of Jesus Christ and explore what they have to give.

A LOOK AT THE LESSON

1. Christmas Mural (5 to 10 minutes)
2. Christmas in Action (5 to 10 minutes)
3. Gifts for Jesus (up to 5 minutes)
4. Christmas Bells (up to 5 minutes)
5. Parade of Bells (up to 5 minutes)
6. Wise Men's Search (up to 5 minutes)
7. Christmas Prayer (up to 5 minutes)

A SPRINKLING OF SUPPLIES

Gather masking tape, large sheets of newsprint, markers, a Bible, photocopies of the "Gifts for Jesus" handout, paper cups, ribbon, glue, jingle bells, yarn, paper clips, self-stick gift bows and chocolate kisses.

THE LIVELY LESSON

1. Christmas Mural

(Before the children arrive, tape large sheets of newsprint to a wall to form a mural. Write "Christmas Is a Time to Give" across the top of the mural. You'll need markers.)

As children arrive, point out the mural and markers. Read the words written across the top of the mural. Quickly sketch a large, simple outline of a stable. Invite children to work together to add drawings of Mary, Joseph, baby Jesus, shepherds, angels and animals.

CHRISTMAS STABLE

Print these words from John 3:16 at the bottom of the mural and read them to the class: "God loved the world so much that he gave his one and only Son."

When the mural is finished, say: **You've done a really good job! Now that you've made this beautiful mural, let's see if we can make the picture come to life!**

2. Christmas in Action

(You'll need a Bible.)

Set up a live Christmas scene by assigning children the following roles:

● To make a stable, have six children stand facing each other with their arms forming an arch.

● To make a manger, have two children kneel facing each other, hold out their arms and grasp hands.

● To make a star, have one child stand on a chair and slowly wave his or her arms.

Have other children take the parts of the innkeeper, Mary, Joseph, shepherds, animals and angels. If you have fewer than 16 children, have two or four children make the stable instead of six. The innkeeper, the shepherds and the angels can also be animals.

Assign roles and have all the children pose in their places. Open your Bible to Luke 2. Then say: **Now sit down and listen carefully to my story. When I mention your part, jump up and take your place or act out what happens. Ready? Here we go!**

Tell the story, pausing to allow children to act it out. Say: **Joseph and Mary traveled to the city of Bethlehem to pay their taxes** (*have Joseph and Mary walk around the room*).

It was a long, tiring journey. By the time they reached the city, they were very tired. Not only that—it was time for baby Jesus to be born. Joseph went to the innkeeper (*have Joseph walk up to the innkeeper*)**, but the innkeeper shook his head. "Sorry," he said. "The only room we have is in the stable"** (*have innkeeper say "Sorry, the only room we have is in the stable"*)**.

Mary and Joseph went to the stable** (*have the children form the stable and have Mary and Joseph walk into it*)**. It was filled with friendly animals** (*have the animals crawl to the stable*)**. The walls kept out the cold wind. There was a manger filled with hay** (*have two children form the manger*)**. And a beautiful star twinkled in the sky above** (*have one child stand on a chair and wave his or her arms*)**.

Joseph and Mary sat down to rest** (*have them sit in the stable*)**. Soon baby Jesus was born! Mary wrapped her baby in warm cloths and laid him on the fresh, sweet hay** (*have Mary pretend to wrap up the baby and lay him in the manger*)**.

There were shepherds nearby on the hillside** (*have the shepherds stand in another part of the room*)**. Angels came to the shepherds and told them baby Jesus had been born** (*have the angel go to the shepherds and say "Jesus has been born"*)**. The shepherds hurried to Bethlehem** (*have the shepherds walk to the stable*)**. When they found the baby in the manger, they knelt down and worshiped him** (*have the shepherds kneel in front of the manger*)**.

When you finish the story, have children give themselves a round of applause.

Then gather everyone together and ask:

● **What's your favorite part of the Christmas story?**

● **If you could be anyone in the Christmas story, who would you be?**

● **How do you think the shepherds felt when angels suddenly appeared in the sky and talked to them?**

● **How do you think God felt**

when baby Jesus was born?

● **How is that like the way you feel when you give a really wonderful gift to someone?**

Say: **When Christmas comes, it's easy to think about what we're going to get. But God wants us to think about what we can give. God gave us his very own son. Now we're going to think about what we can give God this Christmas.**

3. Gifts for Jesus

(You'll need markers and photocopies of the "Gifts for Jesus" handout.)

Distribute markers and photocopies of the "Gifts for Jesus" handout. Say: **Usually we think of gifts being wrapped up in boxes with pretty bows on top. But some of the best gifts don't come in a box. The best gifts often come from our hearts.**

Ask:

● **What gifts don't come in boxes?**

Say: **Sometimes you can give gifts of kindness, like when you help your mom or dad when they're really busy or when you help your teacher straighten up the room or when you cheer up somebody who's sad. Those gifts can't be put in a box!**

Now it's your turn to think of a special gift you can give this Christmas that can't be put in a box. On your paper, draw a picture of you giving someone a gift of kindness.

Allow a few minutes for children to draw. Then have everyone find a partner and explain their pictures to each other.

Say: **When we do kind things for other people, it's like giving a gift to Jesus, because he loves us and he wants us to love others. Write your**

name on the gift tag on your paper to show that you're giving a gift of kindness to Jesus this Christmas.

Help children tape their papers to the wall near the Christmas mural from activity 1.

4. Christmas Bells

(You'll need paper cups, a marker, ribbon, glue, jingle bells, yarn, paper clips and self-stick gift bows. If possible, arrange for two or three teenage or adult helpers for this activity. If you don't have helpers, tie the jingle bells to the yarn before the lesson.)

CHRISTMAS BELLS

Say: **The best part of Christmas is celebrating God's love—the love God showed when he gave us his son and the love that we show by giving gifts of kindness to each other. When it's time to celebrate, there's nothing more fun than bells. We're going to make Christmas bells right now.**

Give each child a paper cup with a small hole poked in the bottom. Have children write their initials on the inside of their cups.

Use these steps to assemble the Christmas bells:

a. Turn the cup upside down. Wrap and glue a length of Christmas ribbon above the rim of the cup.

b. Tie jingle bells to both ends of a 10-inch length of yarn. Fold the yarn in half and poke the fold through the hole in the cup. Slide the fold of the yarn through a paper clip on the top of the cup.

c. Hide the paper clip with a self-stick gift bow on the top of the cup.

When children have finished their bells, have them shake the cups and ring the bells together. Ask:

● **How does the sound of the bells make you feel?**

● **Why are bells a good thing to make at Christmas time?**

Say: **Now that we've made our bells, let's have a celebration!**

5. Parade of Bells

(You'll need the Christmas bells from the previous activity.)

Say: **One gift we can give at Christmas is to tell others about God's love.**

Teach children the following song to the tune of "Jingle Bells."

**Jingle bells, good news tell,
Jesus Christ is born.
Sing the good news everywhere
This happy Christmas morn!**

After children have learned the words to the song, have them march around the room ringing their bells and singing. For more fun, have them parade through the halls ringing and singing.

6. Wise Men's Search

(Before the lesson, hide chocolate kisses around the room.)

Say: **Now that we've done all that singing and ringing, it's time for a treat! But you'll have to find it.**

Ask:

● **Do you remember who searched and searched 'til they found baby Jesus?**

Say: **The wise men followed the star until they found Jesus. Today, you're going to search for your treat—just as the wise men searched for baby Jesus. I've hidden candy around the room. Search for it, but don't eat any until I tell you to. Ready? Go!**

When most of the candies have been found, call the children together.

Ask:

● **How did you feel when you found a piece of candy?**

● **How is that like the way the wise men felt when they found Jesus?**

● **What did the wise men do when they found Jesus?**

Say: **Just as the wise men gave gifts to Jesus, we're going to give gifts to each other. Don't eat any of the candies you found—give them to someone else. They'll give you candy, too. Let's all share so everyone has about the same number of candies.**

Have some extra candy on hand. Give candy to any children who have less than the others.

Ask:

● **How did it feel to share your candies?**

● **How did it feel when your friends shared their candies with you?**

Say: **Christmas is all about giving. It feels good to give! Now let's enjoy our treats together.**

7. Christmas Prayer

To close the lesson, have children gather beside the Christmas mural. Pray: **Dear God, thank you for giving us Jesus. Help us to remember** **that Christmas is a time when we show love to others, just as you showed your love to us. Amen.**

by Lois Keffer

GIFTS FOR JESUS

CONTRIBUTORS

Elaine Friedrich is a director of an elementary-age ministry in Texas.

Maureen Hollen is an elementary school teacher in Colorado.

Janel Kauffman teaches preschoolers and elementary-age children at a Christian school in Florida.

Lois Keffer is Senior Editor of Group Books & Curriculum.

Jolene Roehlkepartain is an editor in Minnesota.

Christine Yount is Editor of CHILDREN'S MINISTRY Magazine.

BRING THE BIBLE TO LIFE FOR YOUR 1ST THROUGH 6TH GRADERS WITH GROUP'S HANDS-ON BIBLE CURRICULUM™

Energize your kids with Active Learning!

Group's **Hands-On Bible Curriculum**™ will help you teach the Bible in a radical new way. It's based on Active Learning—the same teaching method Jesus used.

In each lesson, students will participate in exciting and memorable learning experiences using fascinating gadgets and gizmos you've not seen with any other curriculum. Your elementary students will discover biblical truths and <u>remember</u> what they learn because they're <u>doing</u> instead of just listening.

You'll save time and money too!

While students are learning more, you'll be working less—simply follow the quick and easy instructions in the **Teachers Guide**. You'll get tons of material for an energy-packed 35- to 60- minute lesson. In addition to the easy-to-use **Teachers Guide**, you'll get all the essential teaching materials you need in a ready-to-use **Learning Lab®**. Plus, you'll SAVE BIG over other curriculum programs that require you to buy expensive separate student books—all student handouts in Group's **Hands-On Bible Curriculum** are photocopiable!

Challenging topics each quarter keep your kids coming back!

Group's **Hands-On Bible Curriculum** covers topics that matter to your kids and teaches them the Bible with integrity. Switching topics every month keeps your 1st- through 6th- graders enthused and coming back for more. The full two-year program will help your kids...
- make God-pleasing decisions,
- recognize their God-given potential, and
- seek to grow as Christians.

Take the boredom out of Sunday school, children's church, and youth group for your elementary students. Make your job easier and more rewarding with no-fail lessons that are ready in a flash. Order Group's **Hands-On Bible Curriculum** for your 1st- through 6th- graders today.

Hands-On Bible Curriculum is also available for Toddlers & 2s, Preschool, and Pre-K and K!

TEACH YOUR PRESCHOOLERS AS JESUS TAUGHT WITH GROUP'S *HANDS-ON BIBLE CURRICULUM*™

Hands-On Bible Curriculum™ for preschoolers helps your preschoolers learn the way they learn best—by touching, exploring, and discovering. With active learning, preschoolers love learning about the Bible, and they really remember what they learn.

Because small children learn best through repetition, Preschoolers and Pre-K & K will learn one important point per lesson, and Toddlers & 2s will learn one point each month with **Hands-On Bible Curriculum**. These important lessons will stick with them and comfort them during their daily lives. Your children will learn:
- God is our friend,
- who Jesus is, and
- we can always trust Jesus.

The **Learning Lab®** is packed with age-appropriate learning tools for fun, faith-building lessons. Toddlers & 2s explore big **Interactive StoryBoards**™ with enticing textures that toddlers love to touch. **Bible Big Books**™ captivate Preschoolers and Pre-K & K while teaching them important Bible lessons. With **Jumbo Bible Puzzles**™ and involving **Learning Mats**™, your children will see, touch, and explore their Bible stories. Each quarter there's a brand new collection of supplies to keep your lessons fresh and involving.

Fuzzy, age-appropriate hand puppets are also available to add to the learning experience. These child-friendly puppets help you teach each lesson with scripts provided in the **Teachers Guide**. Cuddles the Lamb, Whiskers the Mouse, and Pockets the Kangaroo turn each lesson into an interactive and entertaining learning experience.

Just order one **Learning Lab** and one **Teachers Guide** for each age level, add a few common classroom supplies, and presto—you have everything you need to build faith in your children. For more interactive fun, introduce your children to the age-appropriate puppet who will be your teaching assistant and their friend. **No student books required!**

Hands-On Bible Curriculum is also available for grades 1–6.

INNOVATIVE RESOURCES FOR YOUR CHILDREN'S MINISTRY

Big Action Bible Skits
Christine Yount

At last—drama that's both exciting *and* easy! Using eight full-color overhead transparencies and ten skits, your elementary children will learn about the Bible as they act out favorite Old Testament Bible stories—without expensive scenery and sets. Simply shine the appropriate overhead on the wall and presto—instant staging!

Encourage learning by helping your children experience Bible stories...and have fun at the same time. Five- to 10-minute skits include...
- Adam and Eve,
- Noah and the Ark,
- Moses and the Exodus,
- Jonah and the Big Fish, and more!

ISBN 1-55945-258-7

Helping Children Know God

A must for anyone who wants to help elementary-age children understand specific attributes of God. Here's active learning at its best—program ideas appeal to all five senses and include suggestions for use in and out of the classroom. You'll help children discover...
- God is loving
- God is all-knowing
- God is faithful
- God is everywhere...and more!

With 140 ideas for helping children know God, this book will be a part of your lesson planning week after week.

ISBN 1-55945-605-1

101 Creative Worship Ideas for Children's Church
Jolene Roehlkepartain

Get your children excited about God with over 100 new, creative ideas for children's worship. Each idea is easy to use and works for children's church, Sunday school, or any place children are gathered to worship God.

You'll discover ideas for...
- prayers
- puppet scripts
- Bible stories
- devotions
- object lessons
- holidays, and more!

Written by children's ministry veteran Jolene Roehlkepartain, this book is jam packed with creative ideas that will help you lead your children in worship meetings that are exciting and meaningful.

ISBN 1-55945-601-9

Order today from your local Christian bookstore, or write:
Group Publishing, Box 485, Loveland, CO 80539.